CGP

GCSE AQA
Biology
For the Grade 9-1 Course

Practice Exam Papers
Instructions & Answer Book

Higher Tier

Pack Two

Inch-perfect exam practice from CGP!

You can't bluff your way through AQA's Grade 9-1 GCSE Biology exams. No chance. What you need is a way of making sure you're 100% prepared.

That's where this brilliant pack from CGP comes in. It contains two full sets of realistic mock exams, so you get used to tackling the types of questions examiners love to ask — all in the comfort of your own home / classroom / private jet.

We've also included full answers and mark schemes for all the papers, so it's easy to check how you're getting on. You'll be ready for anything when the real exams roll around.

What to Expect in The Exams

1) Topics are Covered in Different Papers

For AQA GCSE Biology, you'll sit two exam papers at the end of your course.

Paper	Time	No. of marks	Specification Topics Assessed
1	1 hr 45 mins	100	1, 2, 3 and 4
2	1 hr 45 mins	100	5, 6 and 7

You're expected to know the basic concepts of biology in both papers.

2) You'll be Tested on your Maths...

At least 10% of the total marks for AQA GCSE Biology come from questions on the maths skills you've used in the course. You'll be expected to calculate the mean and range for a set of data, so make sure you know how to do it for your exam.

3) ...and on your Practical Skills

- AQA GCSE Biology contains ten required practical activities that you'll do during the course — but you can also be asked about them in the exams.
- At least 15% of the total marks will be from questions testing practical skills.
- For example, you might be asked to comment on the design of an experiment (the apparatus and methods), make predictions, analyse or interpret results... Pretty much anything to do with planning and carrying out the investigations.

You could be asked about other practical activities as well. So you'll need to be able to apply the skills you've learnt for the required practicals to other experiments.

Marking Your Papers

- Do a complete exam set (Paper 1 and Paper 2).
- Use the answers and mark scheme in this booklet to mark each exam paper.
- Write down your mark for each paper in the table below — each paper is worth 100 marks.
- Find your total for the whole exam (out of a maximum of 200 marks) by adding up your marks from both papers.
- Follow the instructions below to estimate your grade.

	Paper 1	Paper 2	Total mark	Grade
SET A				
SET B				

Estimating Your Grade

- If you want to get a **rough idea** of the grade you're working at, we suggest you compare the **total mark** you got in **each set** to the latest set of grade boundaries.
- Grade boundaries are set for each individual exam, so they're likely to **change** from year to year. You can find the latest set of grade boundaries by going to **www.cgpbooks.co.uk/gcsegradeboundaries**
- Jot down the marks required for each grade in the table below so you don't have to refer back to the website. Use these marks to **estimate your grade**. If you're borderline, don't push yourself up a grade — the real examiners won't.

Total mark required for each grade						
Grade	9	8	7	6	5	4
Total mark out of 200						

- Remember, this will only be a **rough guide**, and grade boundaries will be different for different exams, but it should help you to see how you're getting on.

Published by CGP

Contributor: Alison Popperwell.
Editors: Ciara McGlade, Rachael Rogers, Hayley Thompson.
Proofreader: Philip Armstrong.

Many thanks to Ana Pungartnik for the copyright research.

Clipart from Corel®
Printed by Elanders Ltd, Newcastle upon Tyne.

Text, design, layout and original illustrations
© Coordination Group Publications Ltd. (CGP) 2017
All rights reserved.

Photocopying more than 5% of this book is not permitted, even if you have a CLA licence.
Extra copies are available from CGP with next day delivery • 0800 1712 712 • www.cgpbooks.co.uk

Answers

Set A — Paper 1

1.1 Nucleus, cell membrane, mitochondria, cytoplasm *[1 mark]*

1.2 Subcellular structure: e.g. ribosomes *[1 mark]*
Reason: e.g. because ribosomes are needed for protein synthesis *[1 mark]*.

1.3 To provide them with the energy they need to contract *[1 mark]*.

2.1 Blood is a tissue *[1 mark]*.

2.2 E.g.

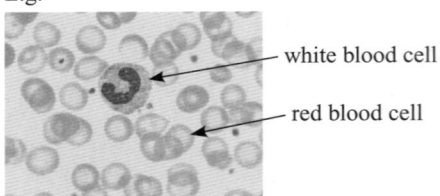

[1 mark for both a white blood cell and a red blood cell correctly labelled]

2.3 E.g. platelets *[1 mark]*

2.4 E.g. excessive bleeding/bruising when injured *[1 mark]*

2.5 Some white blood cells can change shape and engulf pathogens in the blood/carry out phagocytosis *[1 mark]*.
Some white blood cells produce antibodies *[1 mark]*.
Some white blood cell produce antitoxins *[1 mark]*.

2.6 Having more red blood cells means that more oxygen can be carried to the muscles *[1 mark]*. This may improve an athlete's performance during a race as it means there is more oxygen available for aerobic respiration *[1 mark]*. This means more energy can be transferred for muscle contraction *[1 mark]*, allowing the athlete to run faster/run for longer *[1 mark]*.

3.1 How to grade your answer:
Level 0: There is no relevant information. *[No marks]*
Level 1: There is a brief comparison of the defence responses of both plants against pathogens or herbivores. Either the similarities or differences are discussed. *[1 to 2 marks]*
Level 2: There is some comparison of the defence responses of both plants against pathogens or herbivores. Both similarities and differences are discussed. *[3 to 4 marks]*
Level 3: There is a clear and detailed comparison of the defence responses of both plants against pathogens and herbivores. Both similarities and differences are discussed in detail. *[5 to 6 marks]*

Here are some points your answer may include:
Both garden roses and foxgloves have similar methods for protecting themselves against infection by pathogens.
For example, both plants have a waxy cuticle, which provides a barrier to stop pathogens entering.
Also, the cells of both plants will have cell walls that contain cellulose. These will form a physical barrier against pathogens that make it past the waxy cuticle.
However, the garden rose produces antibacterial compounds to kill bacteria on its surfaces, whereas it is not known whether the foxglove is able to do this.
Garden roses and foxgloves have different methods for protecting themselves against damage from herbivores.
Roses have thorns and foxgloves have poisonous stems or leaves. Both thorns and poisonous chemicals will deter herbivores from eating a plant and causing damage.

3.2 digitalis *[1 mark]*

4.1 Blood vessel A: artery
Reason: it has thick walls / thick layers of muscle and elastic in its walls / a small lumen relative to the thickness of its walls. *[1 mark for 'artery' plus correct reason]*
Blood vessel B: vein
Reason: it has thin walls / thin layers of muscle and elastic in its walls / a large lumen relative to the thickness of its walls. *[1 mark for 'vein' plus correct reason]*

4.2 Statins are used to reduce blood cholesterol levels *[1 mark]*, which slows down the rate at which fatty deposits form *[1 mark]* in coronary arteries *[1 mark]*.

4.3 To make sure the drug does not have any harmful effects on the body when it is working normally *[1 mark]*.

4.4 E.g. the patients must be within the same age range / all the same gender / an equal mix of both genders *[1 mark]*.

4.5 To remove any bias *[1 mark]*.

4.6 A substance that's like the drug being tested, but doesn't do anything *[1 mark]*.

4.7 E.g. patients taking a placebo could become very ill without proper treatment *[1 mark]*.

5.1 The spreading out of particles in a solution or gas from an area of higher concentration to an area of lower concentration *[1 mark]*.

5.2 Any two from: e.g. they have a good blood supply *[1 mark]*, which maintains the concentration gradient of gases for diffusion *[1 mark]*. / They have thin walls *[1 mark]*, so gases only have a short distance to diffuse *[1 mark]*. / They have a large surface area *[1 mark]*, so lots of gas molecules can diffuse at once *[1 mark]*.

5.3 E.g. gas exchange would be less efficient *[1 mark]* because the mucus would block parts of the alveoli, reducing their surface area / because thick mucus would increase the distance gases have to diffuse *[1 mark]*.

6.1 It will increase *[1 mark]* because water molecules will move from the area of higher water concentration in the beaker *[1 mark]* to the area of lower water concentration inside the Visking tubing *[1 mark]*.

6.2 E.g. set up the same apparatus with different concentrations of sugar solution inside the Visking tubing *[1 mark]*. Leave the apparatus for a set amount of time/30 minutes *[1 mark]*. Compare the change in volume inside the capillary tube for each solution to determine how the concentration of the sugar solution affected the rate of osmosis *[1 mark]*.

7.1 One molecule of glycerol *[1 mark]* and three molecules of fatty acid *[1 mark]*. *[Allow 1 mark if answer refers to glycerol and fatty acids but the quantities of either are incorrect.]*

7.2 E.g. for keeping its body temperature steady/for keeping warm *[1 mark]*. For muscle contraction/movement *[1 mark]*.

7.3 Any three valid points from: e.g. aerobic respiration takes place in the presence of oxygen, while anaerobic respiration takes place in the absence of oxygen *[1 mark]*. / The products of aerobic respiration in animals are carbon dioxide and water, while the product of anaerobic respiration in animals is lactic acid *[1 mark]*. / Aerobic respiration transfers more energy than anaerobic respiration *[1 mark]*. / Both aerobic and anaerobic respiration are exothermic reactions *[1 mark]*. / Both aerobic and anaerobic respiration use glucose *[1 mark]*.

The question asks you to 'compare' — this means you need to write about the similarities and/or differences between two things. You must write about both aerobic and anaerobic respiration in your answer and you must make it clear that you're comparing the two.

7.4 Add biuret solution to the sample of dog food *[1 mark]*.
If the sample turns from blue to purple, then the food contains proteins *[1 mark]*.

7.5 How to grade your answer:
Level 0: There is no relevant information. *[No marks]*
Level 1: There is a brief explanation of how a dog may digest and absorb a meal containing proteins. *[1 to 2 marks]*
Level 2: There is a clear and detailed explanation of how a dog may digest and absorb a meal containing proteins. *[3 to 4 marks]*
Here are some points your answer might include:
Proteases are digestive enzymes.
They are likely to be produced by the dog's stomach, its pancreas and its small intestine.
Proteases from these locations will break down large, insoluble proteins in the dog's food into small, soluble amino acids.
The products of protein digestion/amino acids will then be absorbed into the bloodstream from the small intestine.

8.1 The iodine solution would remain browny-orange *[1 mark]* rather than turning blue-black *[1 mark]*.

8.2 X = 1000 ÷ 230 = 4.347... = **4.3 s⁻¹** (to 2 s.f.) *[1 mark]*

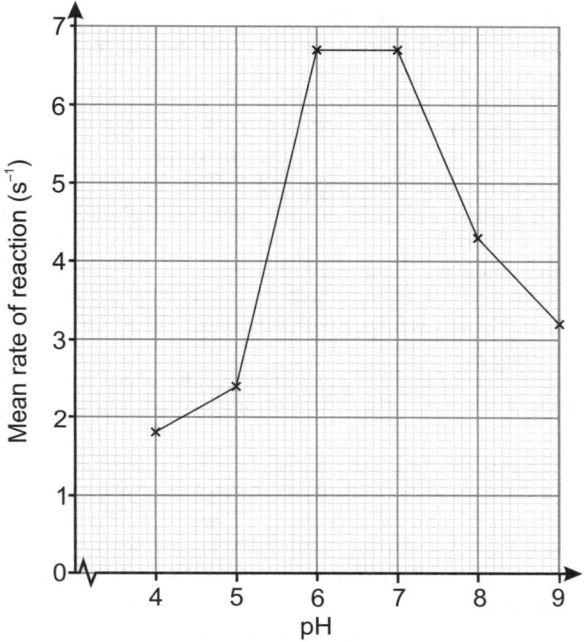

8.3
[4 marks — 1 mark for label and suitable scale for x-axis, 2 marks for all 6 points correctly plotted or 1 mark for 5 points correctly plotted, 1 mark for points joined neatly with straight lines. Allow plotting marks if incorrect answer to 8.2 correctly plotted.]

8.4 Rate of reaction = 4.5 s⁻¹
[1 mark. Accept any answer between 4.4 and 4.6 s⁻¹.]

8.5 E.g. carry out the experiment at pH values between pH 6 and pH 7 *[1 mark]*.

8.6 E.g. the rate of amylase activity decreases as the pH decreases from pH 6 and increases from pH 7 *[1 mark]*.

9.1 E.g. electron microscopes allow us to understand more about mitochondria as their internal structure can be seen in more detail than with a light microscope *[1 mark]*. This is because electron microscopes have a higher magnification/resolution than light microscopes *[1 mark]*.

9.2 Real size = image size ÷ magnification
image size = length of A = 50 mm
Real size = 50 ÷ 14 000 = 0.00357...
= 3.57 × 10⁻³
= **3.6 × 10⁻³ mm** (to 2 s.f.)
[4 marks for the correct answer in standard form to 2 s.f., otherwise 1 mark for A = 50 mm, 1 mark for 0.00357..., and 1 mark for 3.57 × 10⁻³. Allow 3 marks if incorrectly measured length of A used correctly in rest of calculation.]

10.1 The pathogen/protist that causes malaria is carried by a mosquito *[1 mark]*, which acts as a vector *[1 mark]*. The mosquito passes the malaria pathogen/protist between people when it feeds on them/bites them *[1 mark]*.

10.2 E.g. a mouse is injected with an antigen from the pathogen *[1 mark]*. B-lymphocytes that produce antibodies against the antigen are then taken from the mouse *[1 mark]* and fused with tumour cells to create hybridoma cells *[1 mark]*. The hybridoma cells are cloned to produce lots of identical cells which all produce monoclonal antibodies against the pathogen *[1 mark]*. These antibodies are then collected and purified *[1 mark]*.

10.3 How to grade your answer:
Level 0: There is no relevant information. *[No marks]*
Level 1: There is a brief explanation of the effect an anti-malaria vaccine might have on the number of cases of malaria in affected regions. *[1 to 2 marks]*
Level 2: There is a clear and detailed explanation of the effect an anti-malaria vaccine might have on the number of cases of malaria in affected regions. *[3 to 4 marks]*
Here are some points your answer might include:
The vaccine should help to reduce the number of cases of malaria in affected regions.
This is because the anti-malaria vaccine should create immunity to malaria in the people/children who receive it.
The vaccine will work by exposing the person/child to the malaria pathogen, which will stimulate the white blood cells to produce antibodies against the malaria pathogen.
If the person/child who has received the vaccine comes into contact with the malaria pathogen at a later date, their white blood cells should be able to respond quickly to produce the anti-malaria antibodies. This should stop them from getting malaria.
If a large percentage of the population is vaccinated against malaria, it should help to prevent the spread of the disease because there will be fewer people to pass it on.

11.1 E.g. the paper on the lower surface of the leaf got wet, whereas the paper on the upper surface of the leaf did not *[1 mark]*. This is because more water escaped from the lower surface of the leaf *[1 mark]*, suggesting that there are more stomata on this surface / bigger stomata on this surface *[1 mark]*.

11.2 E.g. because the experimental conditions / the humidity/temperature/air movement/light intensity may be different on different days *[1 mark]* which would affect the transpiration rate of the plant, changing the results *[1 mark]*.

11.3 percentage increase = $\frac{\text{final value} - \text{original value}}{\text{original value}} \times 100$
$= \frac{24 - 20}{20} \times 100$
= **20%**
[2 marks for correct answer, otherwise 1 mark for correct working]

11.4 12.00 hours *[1 mark]*. This is when the rate of water uptake, and therefore the rate of transpiration, is greatest *[1 mark]* so the stomata are most likely to be fully open *[1 mark]*.

11.5 E.g. the light intensity/temperature is likely to have increased between 00.00 and 12.00 *[1 mark]*. This will have increased the transpiration rate of the plant and therefore its rate of water uptake, as shown in Figure 8 *[1 mark]*. Between 12.00 and 24.00, the light intensity/temperature is likely to have decreased *[1 mark]*, leading to a corresponding decrease in the rate of water uptake *[1 mark]*.

Set A — Paper 2

1.1 Abiotic factors include soil pH, wind direction and moisture levels. *[1 mark]*
1.2 interdependence *[1 mark]*
1.3 E.g. the number of puffins might decrease *[1 mark]* because there would be fewer herring for them to eat *[1 mark]*.
1.4 E.g. the number of zooplankton might increase *[1 mark]* because there would be fewer herring to eat them *[1 mark]*.
1.5 The thick fur would insulate the polar bear against the cold environment *[1 mark]*. The white fur would camouflage the polar bear against the white snow / help the polar bear avoid predators / help the polar bear sneak up on prey *[1 mark]*.
1.6 E.g. Adaptation: the polar bear has small ears / a low surface area to volume ratio. How it helps survival: having small ears / a low surface area to volume ratio helps reduce heat loss. / Adaptation: the polar bear has large claws/fur on its feet. How it helps survival: these provide the bear with a good grip on the snow/ice. / Adaptation: the polar bear has thick blubber. How it helps survival: the blubber insulates it against the cold.
[2 marks — 1 mark for a correct adaptation, plus 1 mark for correctly explaining how it helps survival.]
2.1 spinal cord *[1 mark]*
2.2 muscle coordination *[1 mark]*
2.3 [diagram of brain with 'medulla' labelled]
[2 marks — 1 mark for 'medulla', 1 mark for correct arrow/line pointing to correct region]
2.4 E.g. [diagram of reflex arc with motor neurone, spinal cord, effector, receptors, hot object labelled]
[1 mark]
2.5 Receptors: to detect the hot object *[1 mark]* and send impulses along the sensory neurone *[1 mark]*.
Effector: to contract *[1 mark]* and move the hand away from the hot object *[1 mark]*.
The effector in this reflex arc is a muscle in the arm.
2.6 Diffusion is the net movement of molecules from an area of higher concentration to an area of a lower concentration *[1 mark]*. The concentration of chemicals is higher in the first neurone than the second *[1 mark]*, so the chemicals will diffuse towards the second neurone *[1 mark]*.
3.1 The malarial parasite reproduces asexually in the human host *[1 mark]* but sexually inside the mosquito *[1 mark]*.
3.2 Level 0: There is no relevant information. *[No marks]*
Level 1: There is a brief explanation of why it is advantageous for the malarial parasite to reproduce either sexually or asexually. *[1 to 2 marks]*
Level 2: There is some explanation as to why it is advantageous for the malarial parasite to reproduce sexually and asexually. *[3 to 4 marks]*
Level 3: There is a clear and detailed explanation as to why it is advantageous for the malarial parasite to reproduce both sexually and asexually. *[5 to 6 marks]*

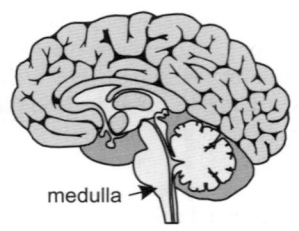

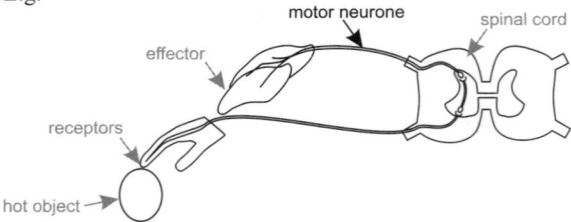

Here are some points your answer may include:
Sexual reproduction produces variation in the offspring, while asexual reproduction does not.
If the environment changes, variation gives a survival advantage by natural selection.
So being able to reproduce sexually makes the malarial parasite population more likely to survive environmental changes than if the parasite only reproduced asexually.
However, asexual reproduction is more energy efficient than sexual reproduction. It is also faster than sexual reproduction. This is because only one parent is needed for asexual reproduction, which means organisms do not need to spend time and energy finding a mate.
So being able to reproduce asexually means that the malarial parasite can rapidly increase its population size when the environmental conditions are favourable.
Being able to reproduce both sexually and asexually allows the malarial parasite to combine the advantages of each method of reproduction.

4.1 E.g. divide each cove into a grid *[1 mark]*. Use a random number generator to select coordinates on the grid *[1 mark]*. Position a quadrat at these coordinates and count the number of dog whelks in the quadrat at that point *[1 mark]*.
4.2 3 *[1 mark]*
4.3 X = (2 + 3 + 3 + 1 + 7 + 8 + 1 + 2 + 5 + 3) ÷ 10
= 35 ÷ 10 = 3.5 = **4** (to 1 s.f.) *[2 marks for correct answer to 1 s.f., otherwise 1 mark for 3.5]*
4.4 E.g. estimated population size = mean number of dog whelks per m^2 × total area of cove in m^2
Mean number of dog whelks per m^2 in cove B = 11 × 2 = 22
Population size of dog whelks in cove B = 22 × 182 = **4004**
[2 marks for correct answer, otherwise 1 mark for correct working]
The quadrats were 0.5 m^2 — so to find the number of dog whelks per m^2, you have to multiply the mean number of dog whelks found in each quadrat by 2.
4.5 Any two from: e.g. cove A may have fewer mussels/barnacles for the dog whelks to feed on. / Cove A may have more crabs/seabirds that eat the dog whelks. / The dog whelks in cove A may be more exposed to changes in abiotic conditions /extremes of temperature/salt concentration. *[2 marks — 1 mark for each correct answer]*
5.1 E.g. the larger the mesh size the greater the rate of decay *[1 mark]*.
5.2 Mass of leaves at 2 months = 30 g.
Mass of leaves at 10 months = 15 g.
Change in mass = 30 − 15 = 15
Rate of decay = 15 ÷ 8 = 1.875 = **1.9 g/month** (to 2 s.f.)
[2 marks for correct answer to 2 s.f., otherwise 1 mark for 1.875]
5.3 The percentage change in the mass of the bags *[1 mark]*.
5.4 the mass of leaves *[1 mark]*
5.5 Any two from: e.g. how deep the bags were buried in the soil. / The distance the bags were buried from the tree. / The approximate size of the leaves. *[2 marks — 1 mark for each correct answer]*
5.6 E.g. increasing the temperature will increase the rate of decay up to a point *[1 mark]* because the enzymes involved in decay work faster at higher temperatures *[1 mark]*. However, if the temperature becomes too hot, the rate of decay slows down *[1 mark]* because the enzymes are denatured / decomposers die *[1 mark]*.

6.1 E.g.

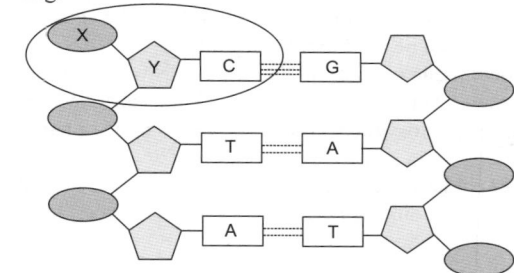

[1 mark]

6.2 X = phosphate *[1 mark]*, Y = sugar *[1 mark]*.
6.3 A pairs with T, so 24% of the bases must be T.
So 24% + 24% = 48% of the bases are either A or T.
100 − 48% = 52% of the bases are either C or G.
52% is shared equally between C and G, so percentage of nucleotides that contain base C = 52% ÷ 2 = **26%**.
[3 marks for the correct answer, otherwise 1 mark for 48% of bases = A or T, and 1 mark for 52% of bases = C or G]
6.4 methionine, asparagine, tryptophan *[1 mark]*
6.5 Because it changes the order of amino acids in the protein *[1 mark]*.
6.6 How to grade your answer:
Level 0: There is no relevant information. *[No marks]*
Level 1: There is a brief explanation of how understanding the human genome can help scientists to trace the migration of certain populations around the world. Some details may be missing or incorrect. *[1 to 2 marks]*
Level 2: There is a clear, detailed and correct explanation of how understanding the human genome can help scientists to trace the migration of certain populations around the world. *[3 to 4 marks]*
Here are some points your answer may include:
All modern humans are descended from a common ancestor who lived in Africa, but humans can now be found all over the world. The human genome is mostly identical in all individuals, but as different populations of people migrated away from Africa, they gradually developed tiny differences in their genomes. By investigating these differences, scientists can work out when the new population split off in a different direction and what route they took.
7.1 E.g. use a protractor that measures in smaller degree/one degree intervals *[1 mark]*.
7.2 E.g. measure the angle at which the seedling bent from the same height on the shoot each time. / Make sure the bulb in the lamp is the same height above the shoot each time. / Set up the experiment in a darkened room so that the shoots only receive light from the lamps and not other sources. *[1 mark]*.
7.3 As the light intensity decreases, the angle at which the seedling bends increases *[1 mark]*.
7.4 Auxin is produced in the tip of the cress seedling *[1 mark]*. The auxin moves towards the shaded side of the tip *[1 mark]*, which makes the cells elongate/grow faster on the shaded side (causing the shoot to bend towards the light) *[1 mark]*.
7.5 Auxin inhibits growth in root cells *[1 mark]*.
7.6 Part of plant: root *[1 mark]*. Advantage: this helps the root to grow down into the soil *[1 mark]*, which anchors the plant / allows it to absorb water/mineral ions from the soil *[1 mark]*.
8.1 It causes the release of an egg from the ovary/ovulation *[1 mark]*.
8.2 Because it secretes several hormones that act on other glands in the body *[1 mark]*, directing them to release hormones *[1 mark]*.

8.3 Hormone: oestrogen *[1 mark]*. Explanation: e.g. the level of hormone B increases at the start of the cycle and reaches its peak just before the release of LH *[1 mark]*. Oestrogen stimulates the release of LH from the ovaries, so hormone B must be oestrogen *[1 mark]*.
8.4 Hormone C is progesterone *[1 mark]*. It maintains the uterus lining *[1 mark]*. If a fertilised egg implants in the uterus wall, the lining needs to be maintained for pregnancy, so the level of hormone C remains high *[1 mark]*.
9.1 To maintain optimal conditions for cell activity and enzyme action *[1 mark]*.
9.2 How to grade your answer:
Level 0: There is no relevant information. *[No marks]*
Level 1: There is a brief explanation of how the body responds to an increase in blood temperature. Some detail may be missing or incorrect. *[1 to 2 marks]*
Level 2: There is a clear, detailed and correct explanation of how the body responds to an increase in blood temperature. *[3 to 4 marks]*
Here are some points your answer may include:
Receptors in the thermoregulatory centre of the brain detect an increase in the temperature of the blood flowing through the brain.
The thermoregulatory centre then sends nervous impulses to effectors, such as blood vessels in the skin, causing them to respond.
Blood vessels in the skin respond by dilating, so that more blood flows close to the surface of the skin. This helps to transfer energy from the skin to the environment, decreasing the body temperature.
Sweat glands in the skin also respond by producing sweat. This evaporates from the skin, transferring more energy to the environment and further decreasing body temperature.
9.3 ADH is released by the pituitary gland *[1 mark]*. ADH causes the kidney tubules to become more permeable to water *[1 mark]*, which causes more water to be reabsorbed back into the blood *[1 mark]*.
10.1 The chromosome number is halved during meiosis (when the gametes are formed) *[1 mark]*. In Figure 13, this is shown by cells with the genotype 'Rr' producing gametes with the genotypes 'R' and 'r' *[1 mark]*. The chromosome number is restored at fertilisation when the gametes fuse *[1 mark]*. This is shown in Figure 13 by gametes with the genotypes 'R' and 'r' producing offspring with the genotypes 'RR', 'Rr' and 'rr' *[1 mark]*.
10.2 3 : 1 *[1 mark]*
10.3 E.g.

	father's gametes	
	r	r
mother's gametes R	Rr	Rr
r	rr	rr

0.5 / 1/2 / 50% of offspring are expected to have smooth hair.
Number of offspring in litter = 6
Expected number of offspring with smooth hair = 6 ÷ 2 = **3**
[5 marks — 1 mark for correctly identifying the mother's/female guinea pig's gametes as Rr, 1 mark for correctly identifying the father's/male guinea pig's gametes as rr, 1 mark for correctly identifying the genotypes of the offspring, 1 mark for correctly calculating the probability of offspring inheriting smooth hair, 1 mark for correctly calculating the expected number of offspring with smooth hair.]

Set B — Paper 1

1.1 E.g. tips of roots *[1 mark]*, tips of shoots *[1 mark]*
1.2 Stem cells in mature plants can differentiate into any type of plant cell *[1 mark]*, whereas stem cells in adult humans can only differentiate into certain types of specialised body cells *[1 mark]*.
1.3 E.g. bone marrow *[1 mark]*
1.4 mitosis *[1 mark]*
1.5 Any two from: e.g. cloning can be used to produce identical plants with the same useful characteristics (e.g. disease resistance). / Cloning can be used to produce lots of plants relatively quickly/cheaply. / Cloning of rare plants could help to protect them from extinction. *[2 marks — 1 mark for each correct answer]*
2.1

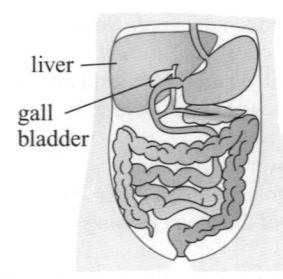

liver
gall bladder

[2 marks — 1 mark for each correct answer]
2.2 Function: bile neutralises the hydrochloric acid which enters the small intestine from the stomach / makes the pH in the small intestine alkaline *[1 mark]*.
Explanation: this is important as digestive enzymes / lipases in the small intestine perform best at an alkaline pH *[1 mark]*.
Function: bile emulsifies fats / breaks fats into tiny droplets *[1 mark]*.
Explanation: this is important as it increases the surface area for lipase to work on / speeds up the rate of fat digestion *[1 mark]*.
2.3 E.g. because the damaged villi are broader/flatter/shorter than the healthy villi *[1 mark]*, and so have a smaller surface area *[1 mark]*. This means fewer food molecules can be absorbed at once *[1 mark]*.
3.1 E.g. Disease: (rose) black spot *[1 mark]*
Explanation: growth is reduced because leaves turn yellow/drop off *[1 mark]* so photosynthesis is reduced *[1 mark]*.
3.2 E.g. the disease may be spread by water/wind (so the infected plant might not have to be close to neighbouring plants to spread the disease to them) *[1 mark]*.
3.3 E.g. use a fungicide on his plants / remove and destroy affected leaves *[1 mark]*.
3.4 How to grade your answer:
Level 0: There is no relevant information. *[No marks]*
Level 1: There is a brief description of the structures of some tissues in a leaf, but little explanation of how they are adapted for photosynthesis. *[1 to 2 marks]*
Level 2: There is some explanation of how the structures of at least three tissues in a leaf are adapted to photosynthesis. *[3 to 4 marks]*
Level 3: There is a clear and detailed explanation of how the structures of at least four tissues in a leaf are adapted to photosynthesis. *[5 to 6 marks]*
Here are some points your answer may include:
The upper surface of the leaf has a waxy cuticle which is waterproof. This helps to prevent water loss from the leaf by evaporation. This is important as water is needed for photosynthesis.
The upper epidermal tissues in the leaf are transparent. This allows light to pass through this tissue to the palisade layer below, which maximises the light available for photosynthesis.
The cells in the palisade mesophyll tissue contain many chloroplasts. Chloroplasts carry out photosynthesis.
The palisade cells are also close to the surface of the leaf and therefore absorb more light for photosynthesis.

The xylem tissue is composed of hollow tubes strengthened by lignin. This enables the tubes to carry water to the cells in the leaf so that it can be used for photosynthesis.
The phloem tissue consists of elongated cells with pores in the end walls. This allows the phloem to transport the sugars produced by photosynthesis out of the leaves to other parts of the plant.
The lower epidermis contains pores called stomata. Stomata allow the carbon dioxide necessary for photosynthesis to diffuse into the leaf.
Guard cells allow the stomata to open and close in response to environmental conditions. For example, when the plant is low on water, the stomata close in order to prevent water loss.
The spongy mesophyll tissue contains many air spaces. This increases the area available for gas exchange and so increases the rate at which carbon dioxide diffuses into the leaf.

4.1 Aerobic respiration uses oxygen and produces carbon dioxide and water. *[1 mark]*
4.2 Metabolism is the sum of all the reactions in a cell or the body *[1 mark]*.
4.3 Flask A shows an overall increase in temperature over the 5 days *[1 mark]*.
4.4 The beans in Flask A were respiring *[1 mark]* and respiration transfers energy to the surroundings (which would have increased the temperature in the flask) *[1 mark]*.
4.5 The boiled beans would have been dead / their enzymes would have been denatured *[1 mark]* and therefore the beans would not have respired *[1 mark]*. This allowed them to act as a control for the experiment *[1 mark]*.
5.1

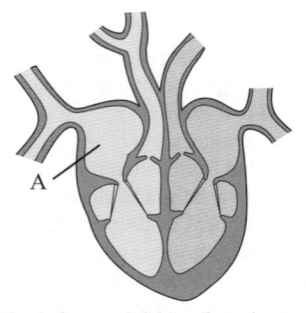

A

[1 mark]
5.2 The left ventricle needs to be stronger/more muscular than the right ventricle *[1 mark]* because it pumps blood all around the body *[1 mark]*, whereas the right ventricle only pumps blood to the lungs *[1 mark]*.
5.3 E.g.
Rate = volume ÷ time
32 750 ÷ 7 = 4678.57... cm^3/min
1 dm^3 = 1000 cm^3
So 4678.57 ÷ 1000 = 4.678... dm^3/min
= **4.7 dm^3/min** (2 s.f.)
[3 marks for the correct answer, otherwise 1 mark for a correct conversion and 1 mark for 4.678...]
5.4 How to grade your answer:
Level 0: There is no relevant information. *[No marks]*
Level 1: There is a brief description of how the blood flows through either the right or left side of the heart. The answer is lacking in detail. *[1 to 2 marks]*
Level 2: There is some description of how the blood flows through both sides of the heart. *[3 to 4 marks]*
Level 3: There is a clear and detailed description of how the blood flows through both sides of the heart.
[5 to 6 marks]
Here are some points your answer may include:
The pulmonary vein brings blood into the left side of the heart from the lungs.
The blood from the pulmonary vein enters the left atrium.
The left atrium contracts, pushing the blood into the left ventricle.

The left ventricle then contracts, pushing the blood out of the heart through the aorta.
The blood then travels around the body before re-entering the right side of the heart through the vena cava.
The blood in the vena cava enters the right atrium first.
The right atrium then contracts, pushing the blood into the right ventricle.
The right ventricle then contracts and pushes the blood through the pulmonary artery.
Both atria contract at the same time and both ventricles contract at the same time, so that the blood on both sides of the heart moves simultaneously.
Valves in the heart prevent the blood from flowing backwards when the chambers contract.

5.5 Treatment: the person could have an artificial pacemaker implanted *[1 mark]*.
Explanation: the pacemaker will produce an electric current that will keep the heart beating regularly *[1 mark]*.

6.1 X: surface area of one side = 0.5 × 0.5 = 0.25
surface area of cube = 0.25 × 6 = **1.5 mm²** *[1 mark]*
Y: 0.1 × 0.1 × 0.1 = **0.001 mm³** *[1 mark]*
Z: 0.54 ÷ 0.027 = **20** : 1 *[1 mark]*

6.2 60 ÷ 12 = **5** times bigger *[1 mark]*

6.3 Cube: A *[1 mark]*
Explanation: Cube A has the smallest surface area to volume ratio so the rate of exchange across its surface would be the slowest *[1 mark]*.

6.4 E.g. warmer water would increase the rate of exchange *[1 mark]* because the diffusing particles would have more energy and therefore move around more *[1 mark]*.

7.1 How to grade your answer:
Level 0: There is no relevant information. *[No marks]*
Level 1: There is a brief description of a method that the student could have used to obtain his results. There is little or no reference to variables that the student could have controlled. *[1 to 2 marks]*
Level 2: There is a thorough description of a method that the student could have used to obtain his results. At least two variables that he should have controlled are given. *[3 to 4 marks]*
Here are some points your answer may include:
Measure a set volume of distilled water into a beaker using a measuring cylinder. This is the 0 mol/dm³ solution.
Measure the same volume of 0.1 mol/dm³ salt solution into a separate beaker. Repeat for the 0.3, 0.5 and 0.7 mol/dm³ salt solutions.
Cut five cylinders of potato of equal size using a cork borer.
Weigh each potato cylinder and place one in each beaker.
Remove the potato cylinders from the solutions after 24 hours.
Dry each potato cylinder with a paper towel.
Reweigh each potato cylinder.
The student should have used the same potato to cut out each cylinder and ensured that the dimensions of the potato cylinder were the same for each beaker.
He should have used the same volume of salt solution or distilled water in each beaker.
He should have stored all the beakers at the same temperature.

7.2 E.g. initial mass = 35 g
4% of 35 = (35 ÷ 100) × 4 = 1.4 g
final mass = 35 − 1.4 = **33.6 g**
[2 marks for the correct answer, otherwise 1 mark for correct working]

7.3 The mass of the potato does not change because osmosis is not occurring / there is no overall movement of water into or out of the potato cells *[1 mark]*.

7.4 E.g. the student could repeat the experiment at concentrations between 0.1 and 0.3 mol/dm³ *[1 mark]* and find at what concentration there is no change in mass of the potato tissue *[1 mark]*.

7.5 No, because some concentrations of salt solution caused the potato tissue to gain mass *[1 mark]*.

7.6 E.g. the concentrated salt solution will cause water to move out of the cells in the weeds by osmosis *[1 mark]*. This will kill the weeds because cells need water for chemical reactions to take place/for photosynthesis *[1 mark]*.

8.1 It means that energy is transferred from the surroundings during the process *[1 mark]*.

8.2 A and B *[1 mark]*

8.3 At this light intensity, the rate of photosynthesis is higher at 0.4% carbon dioxide than at 0.04% carbon dioxide *[1 mark]*. The temperature is the same at both concentrations, suggesting that a carbon dioxide concentration of 0.04% is the limiting factor *[1 mark]*.

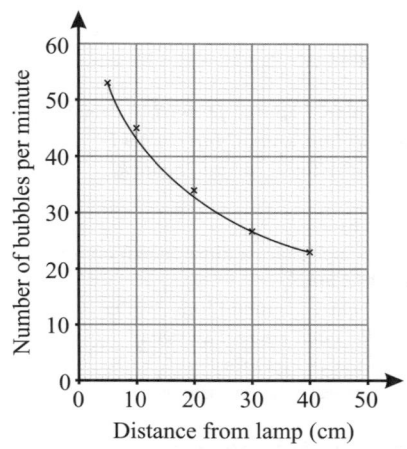

8.4 *[3 marks — 1 mark for a label and suitable scale for the x-axis, 1 mark for correctly plotted points and 1 mark for a correctly drawn curve of best fit]*

8.5 21 cm (allow any answer between 20 and 22 cm) *[1 mark]*
To find the answer, rule directly across from 32 on the y-axis to the curve of best fit. Then rule directly down from the curve to the x-axis and read off the value.

8.6 light intensity = 1 ÷ (40²) = 1 ÷ 1600
= 0.000625 = **6.25 × 10⁻⁴ arbitrary units**
[2 marks for correct answer or 1 mark for 0.000625]

9.1 Because active transport is a process which requires energy *[1 mark]* and mitochondria provide energy for a cell through respiration *[1 mark]*.

9.2 E.g. algae may have competed with the seedlings for the mineral/nitrate ions in the solutions *[1 mark]*, which could have affected the seedlings' growth *[1 mark]*.

9.3 Difference: e.g. the seedling in tube A would be smaller/shorter than the seedling in tube B *[1 mark]*.
Explanation: e.g. tube A was lacking in nitrates *[1 mark]* which are needed (to make proteins) for the plant's growth *[1 mark]*.

9.4 E.g. the solution used in the experiment did not contain enough magnesium ions for the seedlings / the seedlings had used up the magnesium ions in the solutions by this point *[1 mark]*.

10.1 lipases *[1 mark]*, proteases *[1 mark]*

10.2 The optimum temperature could be any value between 40 °C and 60 °C *[1 mark]*. They could only determine the optimum temperature by carrying out the experiment at several temperatures within this range *[1 mark]*.

10.3 At 80 °C some of the bonds holding the enzymes together would have been broken/some of the enzymes would have been denatured *[1 mark]*. This would mean that the shape of the active sites would have no longer fit the shape of the molecules in the stain *[1 mark]*. Therefore, the enzymes wouldn't have been able to break down the molecules in the stain *[1 mark]*.

10

10.4 Any two from: e.g. there was no set mass/volume of egg yolk applied to the pieces of cloth. / There was no set mass of washing powder used. / There was no set volume of water used. / It is unclear how long each piece of cloth was stirred for. / Determining the colour change of the stain was subjective/difficult to do accurately. *[2 marks — 1 mark for each correct answer]*

10.5 The pH of the water would have decreased/would have become more acidic *[1 mark]* because the lipids in the egg yolk would have been broken down into fatty acids/the proteins in the egg yolk would have been broken down into amino acids, which are acidic *[1 mark]*.

Set B — Paper 2

1.1 kingdom, phylum, class, order, family, genus, species *[1 mark]*
1.2 (Carl) Linnaeus *[1 mark]*
1.3 Archaea *[1 mark]*
1.4 E.g. protist / fungus / plant / animal *[1 mark — accept named protist/fungus/plant/animal for 1 mark]*
1.5 E.g. information from the fossil record *[1 mark]*.
1.6 B *[1 mark]*
1.7 Pair of species: L and M
Explanation: These species share a more recent common ancestor than species G and H *[1 mark]*.
2.1 Any two from: light / space / mineral ions / water *[2 marks — 1 mark for each correct answer.]*
2.2 Any two from: food / mates / territory *[2 marks — 1 mark for each correct answer.]*
2.3 E.g. grass → caterpillar → mouse → owl *[2 marks for correct food chain with four trophic levels, otherwise 1 mark if only three trophic levels are correct.]*
2.4 owl *[1 mark]*
Remember, an apex predator is a carnivore that doesn't have any predators.
2.5 Any two from: e.g. adaptation: large/sharp beak. Reason: to grip/eat prey. / Adaptation: large/sharp claws. Reason: to catch/grip prey. / Adaptation: large eyes. Reason: to see small prey more easily. / Adaptation: large wings. Reason: for flying to reach prey *[2 marks — 1 mark for each correct answer. Allow marks for suitable adaptations of an incorrect predator named in 2.4.]*
2.6 Some of the material that an organism eats isn't absorbed/is egested as faeces *[1 mark]*. Some of the material that is absorbed is converted into other substances that are lost as waste *[1 mark]*.
2.7 X = (0.5 ÷ 5.54) × 100 = 9.0252... = **9.03%** (to 3 s.f.) *[2 marks for correct answer, otherwise 1 mark for 9.0252...]*
3.1 A and C *[1 mark]*
3.2 Breed the two varieties of plants together to combine the desired characteristics *[1 mark]*. Select plants from the offspring that show most of the desired characteristics and breed them together *[1 mark]*. Repeat this process over several generations until you get raspberry plants with all the desired characteristics *[1 mark]*.
3.3 E.g. all the plants in the population will have very similar genes / there will be little genetic variation in the population *[1 mark]*. Therefore, if a small number of plants have already been affected by the disease, it's likely that many other plants will also be susceptible and will die *[1 mark]*.
3.4 It contains beta-carotene/a nutrient that is often lacking in the diet of people in developing countries *[1 mark]*.
3.5 Bacterial cells are genetically engineered *[1 mark]* to produce human insulin for the treatment of Type 1 diabetes *[1 mark]*.
4.1 The circular muscles in the iris contracted *[1 mark]* and the radial muscles in the iris relaxed *[1 mark]*.
4.2 It helps to protect the eye/retina from being damaged by the bright light *[1 mark]*.
4.3 stimulus → receptor → coordinator → effector → response *[1 mark]*
4.4 To make sure that all the bacteria were killed *[1 mark]* so that none could survive to mutate *[1 mark]* and form antibiotic-resistant strains *[1 mark]*.
4.5 short-sightedness/myopia *[1 mark]*
4.6 The image of the object is brought into focus in front of the retina *[1 mark]*.
4.7 By changing the amount that light rays entering the eye are bent/refracted *[1 mark]* so that they focus on the retina *[1 mark]*.
4.8 B *[1 mark]*
4.9 E.g. he could wear (hard/soft) contact lenses. / He could have laser surgery on his cornea. / He could have the lens in his eye replaced. *[1 mark]*
5.1 14 cm *[1 mark]*
Remember, the mode is the result that occurs most often.
5.2 X = (17 + 17 + 15 + 16 + 16 + 15) ÷ 6 = **16 cm** *[1 mark]*
5.3 To act as a control / to allow results when listening to music and not listening to music to be compared *[1 mark]*.
5.4 How to grade your answer:
Level 0: There is no relevant information. *[No marks]*
Level 1: There is a brief description of a suitable method but the answer is lacking in detail. There is little or no mention of steps that would ensure the results were valid. *[1 to 2 marks]*
Level 2: There is some description of a suitable method. References are made to several steps that would ensure the results were valid. *[3 to 4 marks]*
Level 3: There is a clear and detailed description of a suitable method. The steps that would need be taken to ensure the results were valid are described in full. *[5 to 6 marks]*
Here are some points your answer may include:
Ask the first volunteer to put on the headphones.
Connect the mp3 player and play music at a fixed, low volume.
Ask the volunteer to sit with their elbow resting on the edge of a table.
Hold the ruler level with the thumb of the first volunteer.
Drop the ruler.
Record the point on the ruler at which the volunteer catches it. This is the distance the ruler has dropped. It should be measured from the same place each time, e.g. the top of the volunteer's thumb.
Repeat the test five times and calculate the mean result.
Repeat the whole experiment three more times with the same volunteer but increase the volume of the music by a set amount each time.
Repeat the whole procedure for the other two volunteers.
Ensure that the headphones used and the music listened to is the same for each repeat and for each volunteer.
Ensure that each volunteer listens to music at the same volumes as the other volunteers.
Carry out the experiments at the same time of day and in the same room.
Use the same ruler each time.
Make sure the volunteers sit in the same position and use the same hand to catch the ruler each time.
Have the same student holding and dropping the ruler and make sure they use the same technique each time.
5.5 50 metres/second *[1 mark]*
6.1 3 minutes 48 seconds = (3 × 60) + 48 = 228 seconds
X = 1000 ÷ 228 = 4.385964... = **4.4 s^{-1}** (to 2 s.f.)
[2 marks for the correct answer to 2 s.f., otherwise 1 mark for 228 seconds]

6.2

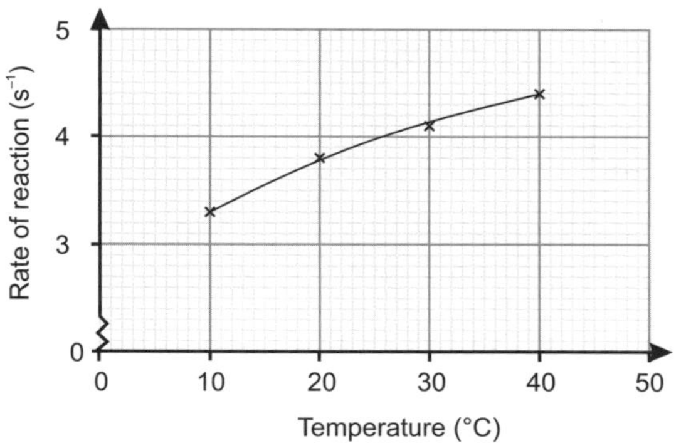

Rate of reaction (s^{-1})
5
4
3
0
0
10
20
30
40
50
Temperature (°C)

[2 marks — 1 mark for all 4 points correctly plotted and 1 mark for a smooth curve of best fit. Allow mark if incorrect answer to 6.1 is correctly plotted.]

6.3 E.g. as temperature increases, the rate at which milk decays also increases ***[1 mark]***.

6.4 The mixture loses its pink colour because it becomes more acidic/its pH falls ***[1 mark]***. This is because the fatty acids produced when fats in the milk are broken down by lipase lower the pH of the mixture ***[1 mark]***.

6.5 E.g. they could have added ice/chilled water to the water bath to reduce its temperature to 10 °C ***[1 mark]***. They could have then regularly monitored the temperature of the water using a thermometer ***[1 mark]*** and added more ice/chilled water if the temperature rose above 10 °C ***[1 mark]***.

6.6 E.g. use a standard colour chart to compare the end point colour with / use a colorimeter to determine the end point ***[1 mark]***.

6.7 E.g. put one test tube B in the water bath at each temperature without adding anything from test tube A ***[1 mark]***. It should not change colour, showing that it was the lipase that caused the colour change ***[1 mark]***. / Use water in place of lipase ***[1 mark]***. Water would not catalyse the reaction, showing that the colour change is due to lipase ***[1 mark]***. / Use boiled lipase ***[1 mark]***. Boiled lipase would be denatured and so could not catalyse the reaction, showing that the colour change is due to the active lipase ***[1 mark]***.

6.8 E.g. microorganisms are responsible for the decay of milk ***[1 mark]***. These may be more likely to survive in regular milk than milk powder, as they need water to survive ***[1 mark]***.

7.1 Amino acids are deaminated ***[1 mark]*** in the liver ***[1 mark]***. Deaminated amino acids form ammonia which is toxic ***[1 mark]***. Ammonia is immediately converted to urea for safe excretion ***[1 mark]***.

7.2 The wrong balance of ions in the blood could mean that too much or too little water is drawn into cells ***[1 mark]*** by osmosis ***[1 mark]***, which could damage cells / stop cells from working properly ***[1 mark]***.

7.3 The glucose concentration of the dialysis fluid is the same as the glucose concentration in healthy blood ***[1 mark]***. This stops too much glucose diffusing out of the blood during dialysis ***[1 mark]***.

7.4 How to grade your answer:

Level 0: There is no relevant information. ***[No marks]***.

Level 1: There is a brief comparison of the advantages and disadvantages of using a dialysis machine and an organ transplant to treat kidney failure, but there is no overall conclusion as to which would be the most beneficial, or there is a conclusion which is inconsistent with the reasoning provided. ***[1 to 2 marks]***

Level 2: There is a clear comparison of the advantages and disadvantages of using a dialysis machine and an organ transplant to treat kidney failure. A conclusion, which is consistent with the reasoning provided, is given as to which would be most beneficial. ***[3 to 4 marks]***

Here are some points your answer may include:
Treating kidney failure with a dialysis machine is very time-consuming for the patient, as dialysis takes several hours and needs to be carried out regularly.
There is a risk of blood clots and infection when undergoing dialysis treatment.
Also, although a dialysis machine can effectively treat kidney failure, it does not cure the condition.
However, there is no waiting list for dialysis treatment, meaning it can be started immediately.
Treating kidney failure with an organ transplant can be risky.
For example, there is a risk of blood clots and infection, and there is a chance that the transplanted organ could be rejected by the patient's immune system.
If the donated organ is coming from a live donor, there are also risks involved for the person donating the organ.
There are long waiting lists for donated organs, meaning that the treatment option isn't available for patients straight away.
However, if a patient has a successful organ transplant, their kidney failure will be cured.
Organ transplants are also cheaper in the long-run than treating kidney failure with dialysis treatment.

Make sure you finish your answer with a conclusion about which option is most beneficial for treating kidney failure. Your conclusion must be supported by the line of reasoning in your answer. E.g. "overall, an organ transplant is more beneficial for treating kidney failure than a dialysis machine — although there are long waiting lists and risks involved with organ transplants, if a patient has a successful transplant they are cured and don't need the inconvenience of having dialysis treatment."

8.1 E.g.

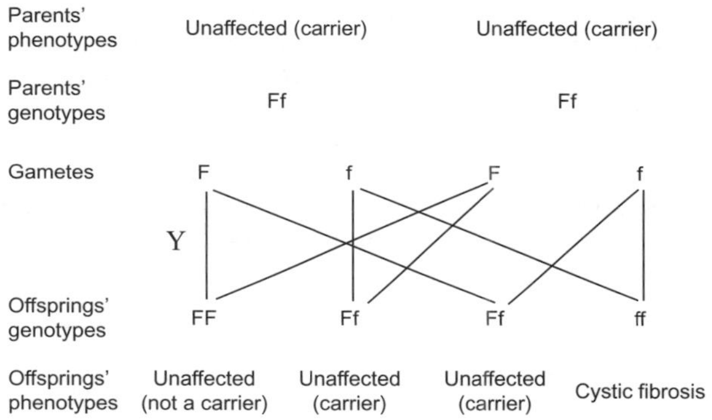

Parents' phenotypes
Unaffected (carrier)
Unaffected (carrier)
Parents' genotypes
Ff
Ff
Gametes
F
f
F
f
Y
Offsprings' genotypes
FF
Ff
Ff
ff
Offsprings' phenotypes
Unaffected (not a carrier)
Unaffected (carrier)
Unaffected (carrier)
Cystic fibrosis

[1 mark for position of Y between gametes and offsprings' genotypes.]

8.2 2 : 1 ***[1 mark]***

8.3 E.g.

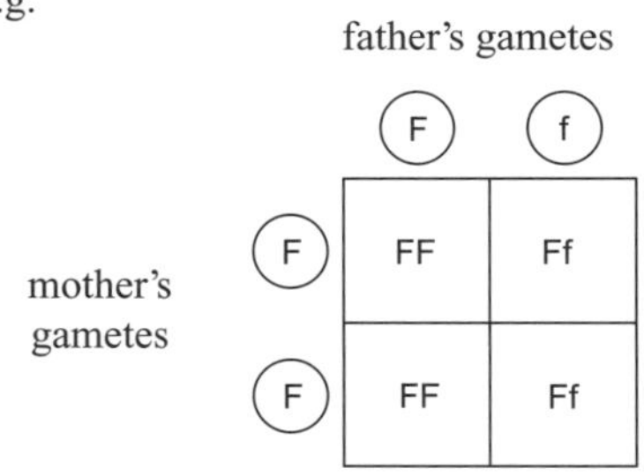

father's gametes
F
f
mother's gametes
F
FF
Ff
F
FF
Ff

Probability of the new baby being unaffected and not a carrier of cystic fibrosis = 50% / 1 in 2 / 0.5

[4 marks — 1 mark for correctly identifying the mother's gametes as FF, 1 mark for correctly identifying the father's gametes as Ff, 1 mark for correctly drawing the Punnett square to show the offsprings' genotypes, 1 mark for correctly stating the probability.]

1018 - 18087

8.4 E.g. both methods prevent pregnancy by releasing progesterone *[1 mark]*. However, the contraceptive implant is effective for longer than the contraceptive injection / the contraceptive implant continuously releases hormones into the body, whereas the contraceptive injection involves hormones being injected directly into the bloodstream in one dose *[1 mark]*.

8.5 Any two from: e.g. sterilisation is a permanent method. / Sterilisation involves surgery. / There is a chance that the tubes cut in sterilisation could rejoin. *[2 marks — 1 mark for each correct answer]*.

9.1 How to grade your answer:
Level 0: There is no relevant information. *[No marks]*
Level 1: There is a brief description of how a protein is synthesised but the answer is lacking in detail. *[1 to 2 marks]*
Level 2: There is a clear, detailed description of how a protein is synthesised. *[3 to 4 marks]*
Here are some points your answer may include:
The DNA in the gene contains bases.
Each sequence of three bases codes for a different amino acid.
An mRNA molecule copies the code from the DNA in the nucleus.
The mRNA molecule carries the code out of the nucleus to a ribosome in the cytoplasm.
The code is used as a template.
Carrier molecules bring amino acids to the ribosome in the correct order.
The amino acids are joined together to form a protein.

9.2 The mutation may alter the order of amino acids that are coded for *[1 mark]*. A different order of amino acids may alter the shape of the protein that is made *[1 mark]*. This may mean that the shape of the enzyme's active site is changed, so its substrate may no longer bind to it *[1 mark]*. This would mean that the enzyme wouldn't function as it should, which may affect the phenotype of the organism *[1 mark]*.

9.3 Non-coding sections of DNA can switch genes on and off *[1 mark]*. So a mutation in a non-coding section of DNA may affect whether or not a gene is expressed, which could affect the phenotype of an organism *[1 mark]*.

GCSE Biology

Set A Paper 1

Higher Tier

In addition to this paper you should have:
- A ruler.
- A calculator.

Centre name				
Centre number				
Candidate number				

Surname
Other names
Candidate signature

Time allowed:
- 1 hour 45 minutes

Instructions to candidates
- Write your name and other details in the spaces provided above.
- Answer **all** questions in the spaces provided.
- Do all rough work on the paper.
- Cross out any work you do not want to be marked.

Information for candidates
- The marks available are given in brackets at the end of each question.
- There are 100 marks available for this paper.
- You are allowed to use a calculator.
- You should use good English and present your answers in a clear and organised way.
- For Questions 3.1, 7.5 and 10.3 ensure that your answers have a clear and logical structure, include the right scientific terms, spelt correctly and include detailed, relevant information.

Advice to candidates
- In calculations show clearly how you worked out your answers.

For examiner's use

Q	Attempt Nº 1	2	3	Q	Attempt Nº 1	2	3
1				7			
2				8			
3				9			
4				10			
5				11			
6							
				Total			

Answer **all** questions in the spaces provided

1 Cells are the basic working unit of life.

1.1 Which subcellular structures would be found in **both** plant and animal cells?
Tick **one** box.

☐ Mitochondria, permanent vacuole, cytoplasm, nucleus

☐ Cytoplasm, chloroplasts, cell membrane, mitochondria

☐ Nucleus, cell membrane, mitochondria, cytoplasm

☐ Cell membrane, cell wall, nucleus, mitochondria

[1 mark]

The human body contains many specialised cell types.
The structure of each cell type varies according to its function.

1.2 Some cells in the salivary glands continually make a protein-containing substance called mucus.

Suggest **one** type of subcellular structure that you would expect to find a lot of in these mucus-producing cells. Give a reason for your answer.

Subcellular structure: ....

Reason: ....

....
[2 marks]

1.3 Cells in the muscles contain many mitochondria.

Suggest why it is an advantage for cells in the muscles to contain many mitochondria.

....

....
[1 mark]

2 **Figure 1** shows a photograph of some human blood cells.

Figure 1

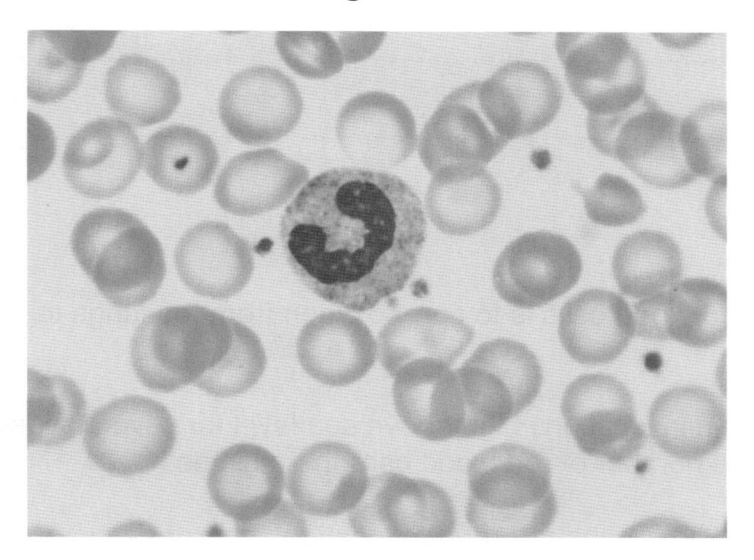

2.1 Which of the following statements about blood is correct?
Tick **one** box.

☐ Blood is a cell.

☐ Blood is a tissue.

☐ Blood is an organ.

☐ Blood is an organ system.

[1 mark]

2.2 Label a red blood cell and a white blood cell on **Figure 1**.

[1 mark]

2.3 Name **one** component of blood that is responsible for blood clotting.

....
[1 mark]

2.4 Suggest **one** symptom that a person might suffer from if they do not have enough of the blood component you named in question **2.3**.

....
[1 mark]

Question 2 continues on the next page

White blood cells help the body to fight infection.

2.5 Give **three** ways in which white blood cells are adapted to perform their function.

1. ....

2. ....

3. ....
[3 marks]

The function of red blood cells is to carry oxygen from the lungs to all cells in the body.

2.6 Some athletes train in locations high above sea level for several weeks before a race. This increases the number of red blood cells the athletes have.

Even once the athletes have returned to locations nearer sea level, their red blood cell count can remain high for many days.

Suggest how training in locations high above sea level might improve an athlete's performance in a race.

....

....

....

....

....
[4 marks]

3.1 **Table 1** shows some information about two types of plant.

Table 1

	Garden rose	Foxglove
Waxy cuticle present?	Yes	Yes
Bark present?	No	No
Thorns present?	Yes, on stems	No
Antibacterial compounds produced?	Yes	Not known
Poisonous stems/leaves?	Not usually	Yes

Using the information in **Table 1** and your own knowledge of plant defences, compare how garden roses and foxgloves defend themselves against:

- infection by pathogens,
- damage from herbivores.

[6 marks]

Question 3 continues on the next page

Many plant defence chemicals have formed the basis of modern medicines.

3.2 Name a drug that has been developed from a chemical found in foxgloves.

....

[1 mark]

4 Blood flows around the human body in blood vessels.
Problems with the blood vessels can lead to disease, such as coronary heart disease.
People are often prescribed medications to treat these diseases.

Figure 2 shows two different types of blood vessel.

Figure 2

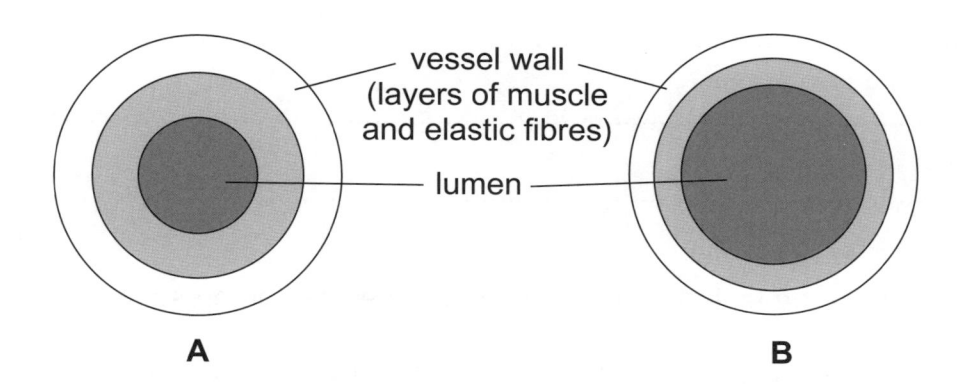

4.1 Name the type of blood vessel represented by **A** and **B** in **Figure 2**.
Give a reason for each of your choices.

Blood vessel A: ....

Reason: ....

Blood vessel B: ....

Reason: ....
[2 marks]

Question 4 continues on the next page

A man is diagnosed with high blood cholesterol levels.
His doctor tells him that he is at risk of developing coronary heart disease.
The man is prescribed statins.

4.2 Explain how statins could reduce the man's risk of developing coronary heart disease.

....

....

....

....
[3 marks]

New drugs have to be tested and trialled before they can be prescribed to patients.

4.3 Explain why clinical trials are always carried out on healthy volunteers before patients.

....

....
[1 mark]

If the results on healthy volunteers are satisfactory, the drug can be tested on patients with the illness that the drug is designed to treat.

Patients are randomly put into two groups — a test group and a control group. The test group is given the new drug and the control group is given a placebo.

4.4 Suggest **one** variable that must be controlled in both groups so that a valid comparison of the results can be made.

....
[1 mark]

4.5 Why is it important that the patients are **randomly** put into groups?

....
[1 mark]

4.6 Explain what is meant by the term 'placebo'.

....

....
[1 mark]

4.7 Suggest **one** reason why it may sometimes be unethical to prescribe a placebo to patients in a control group.

....

....
[1 mark]

Turn over for the next question

5 Gas exchange takes place via diffusion.

Leave blank

5.1 Which of the following is the correct definition of diffusion?
Tick **one** box.

- [ ] The movement of gas molecules in any direction.
- [ ] The spreading out of particles in a solution or gas from an area of higher concentration to an area of lower concentration.
- [ ] The spreading out of particles in a solution or gas from an area of lower concentration to an area of higher concentration.
- [ ] The movement of substances from a more dilute solution to a more concentrated solution, which requires energy.

[1 mark]

Figure 3 shows some alveoli in the human lungs.

Figure 3

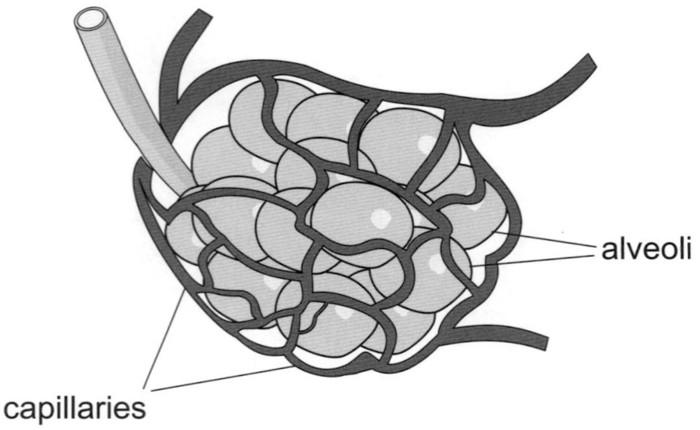

The alveoli are adapted for efficient gas exchange.

5.2 Give **two** ways in which the alveoli are adapted to carry out the process of gas exchange.
Explain how each of these adaptations improves the efficiency of gas exchange.

1. ....

....

2. ....

....

[4 marks]

5.3 Cystic fibrosis is a genetic disorder of cell membranes. It results in the body producing a lot of thick, sticky mucus in the air passages and alveoli.

Explain what effect cystic fibrosis is likely to have on gas exchange.

....

....

....
[2 marks]

Turn over for the next question

6 A student is investigating osmosis using Visking tubing.
Visking tubing is a partially permeable membrane.
Water can pass through Visking tubing, but large sugar molecules cannot.

Figure 4 shows the student's apparatus at the start of her investigation.

Figure 4

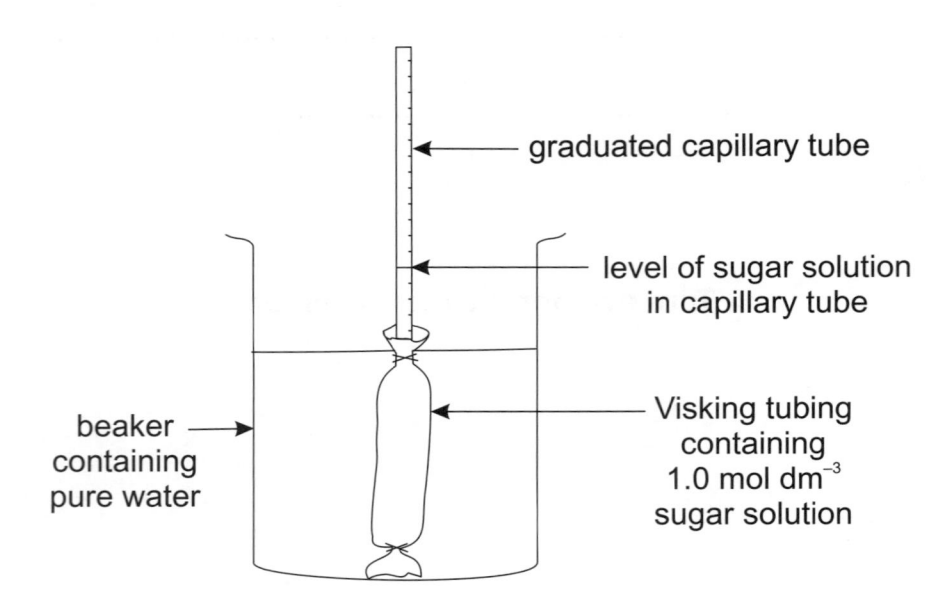

- graduated capillary tube
- level of sugar solution in capillary tube
- beaker containing pure water
- Visking tubing containing 1.0 mol dm^{-3} sugar solution

The student leaves the apparatus for 30 minutes.

6.1 Suggest what will happen to the volume of the sugar solution inside the capillary tube during this time period.
Explain your answer in terms of osmosis.

....

....

....

....

[3 marks]

6.2 Suggest how the student could modify her experiment to investigate the effect of changing the concentration gradient on the rate of osmosis.

....
....
....
....
....

[3 marks]

Turn over for the next question

7 **Figure 5** shows a dog.

Figure 5

Respiration transfers energy from the dog's food to the cells in its body.

Some of the energy transferred by respiration is used to build up larger molecules from smaller molecules.

7.1 Describe which smaller molecules make up a lipid molecule.

....

....
[2 marks]

7.2 Apart from building up larger molecules from smaller molecules, give **two** other examples of how a dog uses the energy transferred during respiration.

1. ....

2. ....
[2 marks]

Respiration can take place aerobically or anaerobically.

7.3 Compare aerobic and anaerobic respiration in animals.

....

....

....

....

....
[3 marks]

Dog food contains a mix of essential nutrients, including protein.

7.4 A student prepared a sample of dog food for testing.
Describe how the student could test for the presence of proteins in the prepared sample.

....

....

....
[2 marks]

7.5 Use your knowledge of digestive enzymes to explain how a dog may digest and absorb a meal containing proteins.

....

....

....

....

....

....
[4 marks]

Turn over for the next question

Turn over ▶

8 The enzyme amylase breaks down starch into simple sugars.

A student investigated the effect of pH on the rate at which amylase breaks down starch. This is the method she used:

1. Amylase and starch solution were added to six test tubes, each of which contained a different pH buffer solution.
2. Spotting tiles were prepared with one drop of iodine solution in each well.
3. Every 30 seconds, a sample of the amylase and starch solution was removed from the test tube and placed in a well on one of the spotting tiles.
4. The colour of the solution in the well was observed.
5. When all the starch had been broken down, the time was recorded.
6. The experiment was repeated three times for each of the six solutions.
7. A mean time and rate of reaction was calculated for each solution.

The results are shown in **Table 2**.

Table 2

pH of buffer solution	Time taken for starch to be broken down by amylase (s)				Mean rate of reaction (s^{-1})
	Repeat 1	Repeat 2	Repeat 3	Mean	
4	510	600	570	560	1.8
5	420	450	390	420	2.4
6	150	120	180	150	6.7
7	180	120	150	150	6.7
8	240	210	240	230	X
9	330	270	330	310	3.2

8.1 Explain how the student would have known when all the starch had been broken down by the amylase.

....

....
[2 marks]

Leave blank

8.2 Calculate the value of **X** in **Table 2**.

Use the equation:

$$\text{rate of reaction} = \frac{1000}{\text{time}}$$

Give your answer to 2 significant figures.

X = ... s^{-1}

[1 mark]

8.3 Complete **Figure 6** using data from **Table 2** and your answer to **8.2**.

- Complete the *x*-axis. Include a label and use a suitable scale.
- Plot the mean rate of reaction for each pH value.
- Join the points with straight lines.

Figure 6

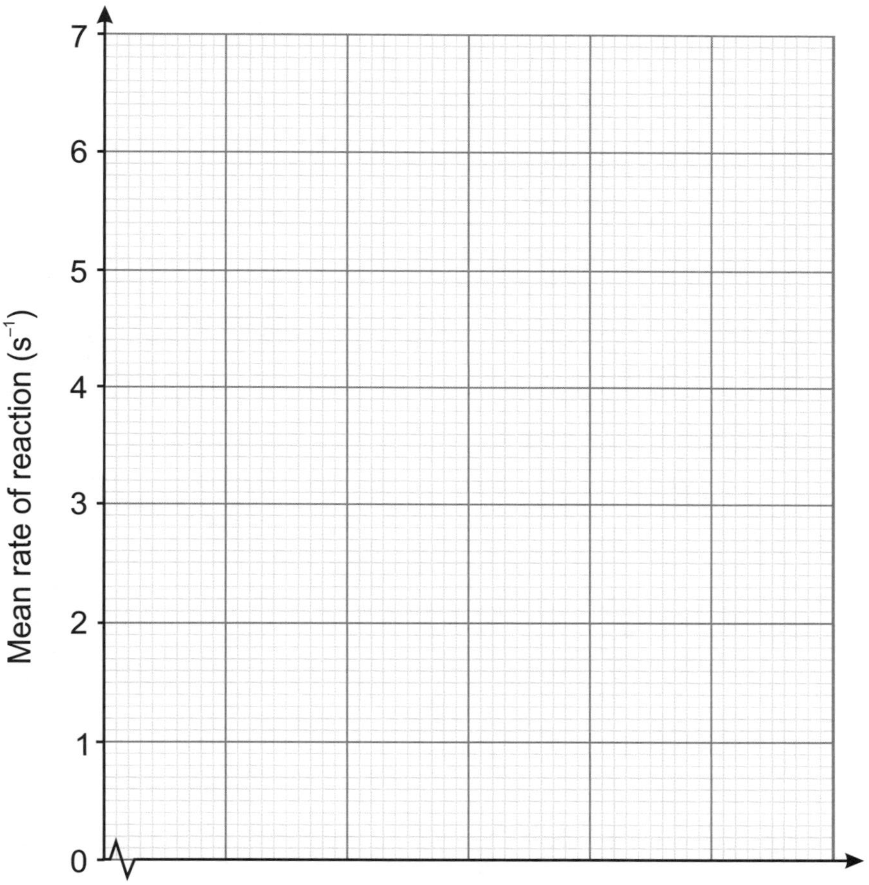

[4 marks]

8.4 Use your graph in **Figure 6** to estimate the rate of reaction at **pH 5.5**.

Rate of reaction = ... s^{-1}

[1 mark]

Question 8 continues on the next page

Turn over ▶

8.5 The results for the mean rate of reaction at pH 6 and 7 are the same. Suggest how the experiment could be improved to determine the optimum pH for amylase more accurately.

....

....
[1 mark]

8.6 Give a conclusion that can be drawn from the results about the effect of pH on the rate of amylase activity.

....

....
[1 mark]

9 Mitochondria were first observed using light microscopes in the 1800s. They were first observed using an electron microscope in the 1950s.

9.1 Suggest how electron microscopes have increased our understanding of mitochondria. Give a reason for your answer.

....

....

....

....
[2 marks]

Figure 7 shows a mitochondrion as seen with an electron microscope.

Figure 7

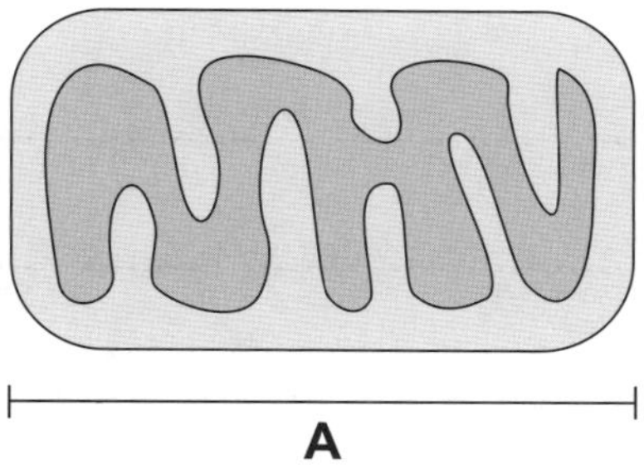

A is the image length.

9.2 The mitochondrion in **Figure 7** was viewed under a magnification of × 14 000. Calculate the real size of this mitochondrion.
Use the formula:

$$\text{magnification} = \frac{\text{image size}}{\text{real size}}$$

Give your answer in standard form to 2 significant figures.

real size = ... mm
[4 marks]

Turn over for the next question

10 In 2015, there were approximately 438 000 deaths from malaria worldwide. Most deaths occurred among children living in sub-Saharan Africa.

10.1 Explain how malaria is spread from person to person.

....

....

....

....

[3 marks]

Malaria is currently diagnosed using a blood test.
Some blood tests for malaria use monoclonal antibodies against the malaria pathogen.

10.2 Describe how monoclonal antibodies against a particular pathogen are made.

....

....

....

....

....

....

....

....

[5 marks]

A vaccine has been developed that provides some protection against malaria in young children. So far, it is the only vaccine available against the disease.

10.3 Explain what impact an anti-malaria vaccine might have on the number of cases of malaria in affected regions.

....
....
....
....
....
....
....
....

[4 marks]

Turn over for the next question

11 Plants lose water through the stomata in their leaves.

A student set up an experiment to show that more water is lost from the lower surface of a leaf than from the upper surface.

He used cobalt chloride paper in his experiment.
This paper is blue when it is dry and pink when it is wet.

This is the method he used:

1. He took a potted plant and taped a piece of dry cobalt chloride paper to the upper surface of one of the plant's leaves.
2. He taped a second piece of paper to the lower surface of the same leaf.
3. He left the plant for 5 minutes.
4. He observed the colour of the pieces of cobalt chloride paper.

The results of the experiment are shown in **Table 3**.

Table 3

	Colour of paper at start of experiment	Colour of paper after 5 minutes
Upper surface of leaf	blue	blue
Lower surface of leaf	blue	pink

11.1 Suggest an explanation for the results shown in **Table 3**.

....

....

....

....
[3 marks]

11.2 The student repeated the experiment on a different day.
This time, neither piece of cobalt chloride paper turned pink after 5 minutes.
Suggest why the results of this experiment may be different on different days.

....

....

....
[2 marks]

It is assumed that water loss from the leaves of a plant is directly proportional to water uptake from the roots.

An investigation was carried out to assess the rate of water uptake by a plant over a 24-hour period. The results are shown in **Figure 8**.

Figure 8

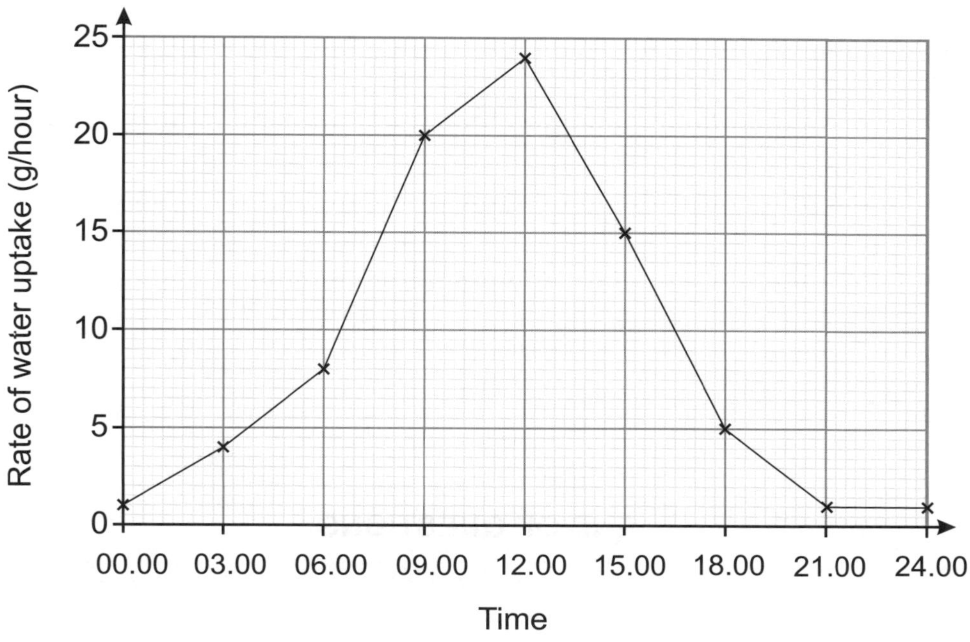

11.3 Use **Figure 8** to calculate the percentage increase in the rate of water uptake between 09.00 hours and 12.00 hours.

percentage increase = ... %

[2 marks]

Stomata are small. It is difficult to accurately measure their diameter unless they are fully open.

11.4 Use **Figure 8** to suggest what time of day it would be best to measure the diameter of stomata on leaves. Give a reason for your suggestion.

....

....

....

....

[3 marks]

Question 11 continues on the next page

Turn over ▶

Leave blank

11.5 Suggest an explanation for the changes in the rate of water uptake shown in **Figure 8**.

[4 marks]

END OF QUESTIONS

GCSE Biology

Set A Paper 2
Higher Tier

CGP Practice Exam Paper GCSE Biology

In addition to this paper you should have:
- A ruler.
- A calculator.

Centre name

Centre number

Candidate number

Surname

Other names

Candidate signature

Time allowed:
- 1 hour 45 minutes

Instructions to candidates
- Write your name and other details in the spaces provided above.
- Answer **all** questions in the spaces provided.
- Do all rough work on the paper.
- Cross out any work you do not want to be marked.

Information for candidates
- The marks available are given in brackets at the end of each question.
- There are 100 marks available for this paper.
- You are allowed to use a calculator.
- You should use good English and present your answers in a clear and organised way.
- For Questions 3.2, 6.6 and 9.2 ensure that your answers have a clear and logical structure, include the right scientific terms, spelt correctly and include detailed, relevant information.

Advice to candidates
- In calculations show clearly how you worked out your answers.

For examiner's use

Q	Attempt N° 1	2	3	Q	Attempt N° 1	2	3
1				6			
2				7			
3				8			
4				9			
5				10			
				Total			

Answer all questions in the spaces provided

1 An ecosystem is affected by both biotic and abiotic factors.

1.1 Which of the following statements is correct?
Tick **one** box.

☐ Biotic factors include soil pH, wind direction and moisture levels.

☐ Abiotic factors include pathogens, predators and temperature.

☐ Abiotic factors include soil pH, wind direction and moisture levels.

☐ Biotic factors include pathogens, predators and temperature.

[1 mark]

Each species in a community depends on other species for things such as food and shelter.

1.2 What term is used to describe this type of relationship?

....
[1 mark]

Figure 1 shows some organisms within a coastal community.

Figure 1

Puffin   Herring   Zooplankton

Puffins feed on the herring. The herring feed on the zooplankton.

1.3 Suggest what effect the removal of a large number of herring may have on the number of **puffins** in the community. Explain your answer.

....

....

....
[2 marks]

Leave blank

1.4 Suggest what effect the removal of a large number of herring may have on the number of **zooplankton** in the community. Explain your answer.

....

....

....
[2 marks]

Organisms are adapted to the abiotic and biotic conditions in which they live.

Polar bears live in the Arctic where conditions are very cold. **Figure 2** shows a polar bear. Polar bears have several adaptations that enable them to live successfully in the Arctic.

Figure 2

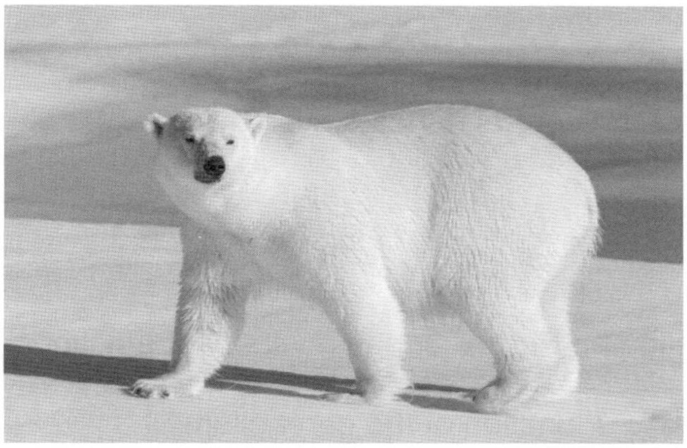

1.5 Suggest **two** benefits of the polar bear having a thick covering of white fur.

1. ....

2. ....
[2 marks]

1.6 Apart from its fur, suggest **one** other structural adaptation that the polar bear has to living in Arctic conditions.
Suggest how this adaptation helps the polar bear to survive.

Adaptation: ....

How it helps survival: ....

....
[2 marks]

Turn over for the next question

Turn over ▶

2 **Figure 3** shows a diagram of the human brain.

Figure 3

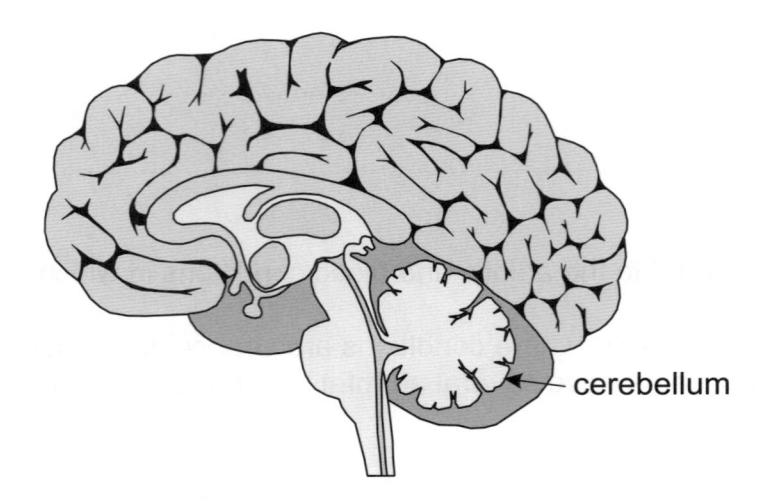

— cerebellum

2.1 The brain makes up part of the central nervous system.
Name the other part of the central nervous system.

....
[1 mark]

The cerebellum, labelled on **Figure 3**, has a variety of functions.

2.2 Which of the following is a function of the cerebellum?
Tick **one** box.

☐ intelligence

☐ memory

☐ consciousness

☐ muscle coordination

[1 mark]

2.3 On **Figure 3**, name and label the region of the brain that controls unconscious activities.

[2 marks]

Reflex actions do not involve the conscious part of the brain.

A boy touches a hot object with his finger and quickly moves his finger away. **Figure 4** shows the reflex arc involved in this response.

Figure 4

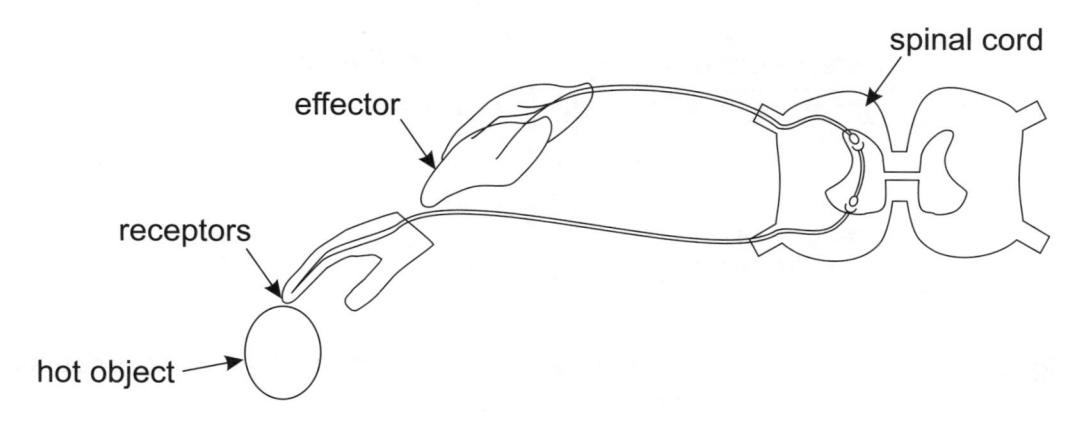

2.4 Label the motor neurone on **Figure 4**.

[1 mark]

2.5 Explain the roles of the receptors and effector shown in **Figure 4**.

Receptors: ....

....

Effector: ....

....

[4 marks]

Question 2 continues on the next page

Figure 5 shows a synapse (a connection between two neurones). The nerve impulse is transferred across the synapse by chemicals which travel by **diffusion**.

Figure 5

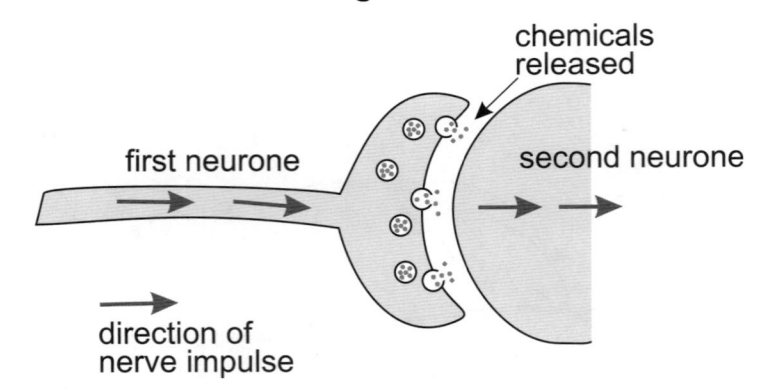

2.6 Use **Figure 5** and your knowledge of diffusion to suggest why the nerve impulse travels from the first neurone to the second neurone.

....
....
....
....

[3 marks]

3 Most organisms reproduce by either sexual or asexual reproduction.

Some organisms can reproduce using both sexual and asexual reproduction.

3.1 Describe how both sexual and asexual reproduction are involved in the life cycle of the malarial parasite.

....

....

....
[2 marks]

3.2 Explain why it is advantageous for the malarial parasite to be able to reproduce both sexually and asexually.

....

....

....

....

....

....

....

....

....

....

....
[6 marks]

Turn over for the next question

4 Dog whelks are a type of snail that live on the seashore.
They feed on mussels and barnacles. They are eaten by crabs and seabirds.

Dog whelks tend to live in the mid-shore area, where they spend most of their time underwater. This helps to protect them against changes in abiotic conditions, such as temperature and the salt concentration of the environment.

A marine biologist used quadrats, each with an area of 0.5 m², to investigate the number of dog whelks living in two different rocky coves (cove **A** and cove **B**).

The biologist counted the number of dog whelks in 10 randomly positioned quadrats in each cove. Her results are shown in **Table 1**.

Table 1

Quadrat Number	Cove A	Cove B
1	2	12
2	3	12
3	3	16
4	1	12
5	7	9
6	8	12
7	1	5
8	2	12
9	5	13
10	3	11
Mean	**X**	**11**

4.1 Describe a method that the biologist could have used to ensure her sampling was random.

....

....

....

....
[3 marks]

4.2 What is the modal number of dog whelks in cove **A**?
Tick **one** box.

☐ 1

☐ 2

☐ 3

☐ 5

[1 mark]

4.3 Calculate the value of **X** in **Table 1**.
Give your answer to 1 significant figure.

X = ...
[2 marks]

Cove A is 150 m². Cove B is 182 m².
The estimated population size of dog whelks in cove **A** is 1200.

4.4 Estimate the population size of dog whelks in cove **B**.

Population size of dog whelks in cove B = ...
[2 marks]

4.5 Suggest **two** reasons why there might be a difference in the population size of dog whelks in the two coves.

1. ....

....

2. ....

....
[2 marks]

Turn over for the next question

5 A group of students investigated the process of decomposition.
They decided to measure the change in the mass of leaves over one year.
They predicted that as the leaves decayed, their mass would decrease.
This is the method they used:

1. The students collected a number of leaves from an oak tree growing on their school field.
2. They then placed an equal number of leaves in three nylon bags, each with a different mesh size.
3. The students weighed each bag, recorded the mass, and then buried it in the soil near the oak tree.
4. Every four months for one year, the students dug up the bags and allowed them to dry before reweighing them.
5. The students then returned the bags to the soil.

Figure 6 shows a mesh bag similar to those used in the investigation.

Figure 6

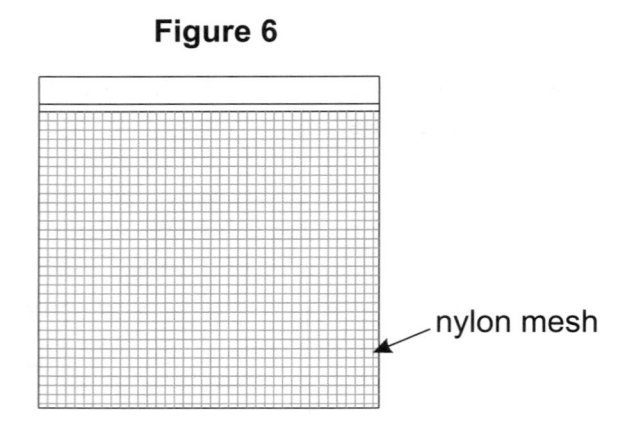

Figure 7 shows the students' results.

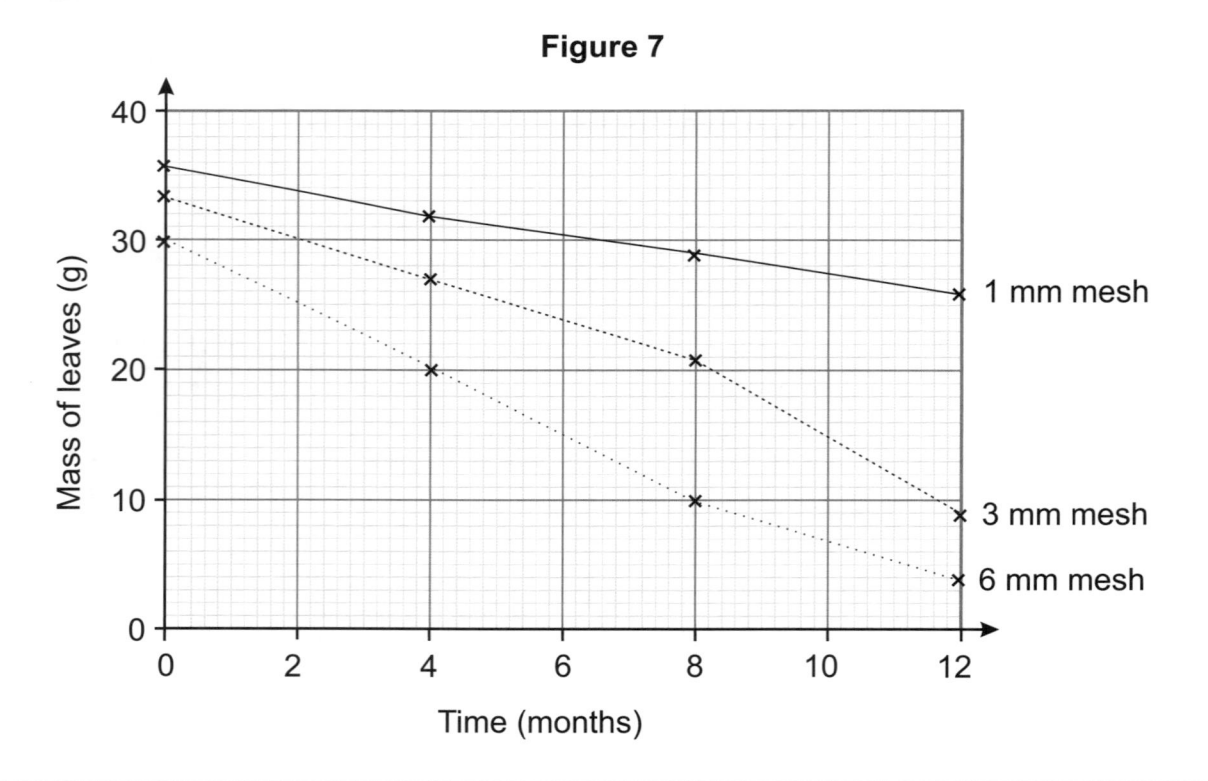

Figure 7

5.1 Use the results in **Figure 7** to give **one** conclusion about the effect of mesh size on the rate of decay.

....

....
[1 mark]

5.2 Use **Figure 7** to determine the rate of decay in the bag with a mesh size of 3 mm between months 2 and 10.
Give your answer to 2 significant figures.

Rate of leaf decay = ... g/month
[2 marks]

5.3 At the start of the experiment, each bag of leaves had a different mass.
What should the students have calculated so that the results could have been compared fairly?

....

....
[1 mark]

5.4 Give the dependent variable in this investigation.

....
[1 mark]

5.5 Give **two** variables that should have been controlled in the investigation.

1. ....

2. ....
[2 marks]

Question 5 continues on the next page

5.6 The rate of decay of biological material is affected by a number of environmental factors, including oxygen, water availability and temperature.

Explain how the rate of decay is affected by temperature.

....

....

....

....

....

[4 marks]

6 Figure 8 shows part of a DNA molecule.

Figure 8

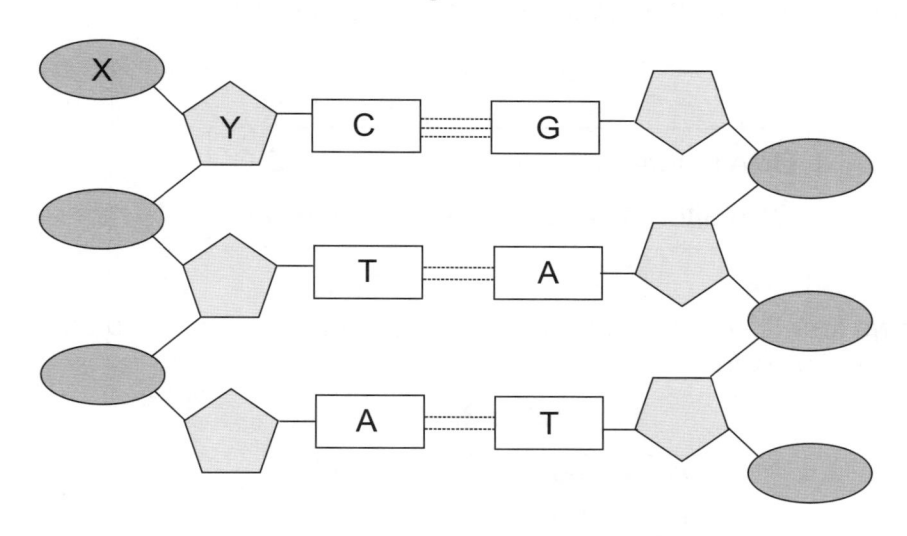

DNA is a polymer made up of lots of repeating units called nucleotides.

6.1 On **Figure 8**, draw a ring around **one** nucleotide.
[1 mark]

6.2 Name the **two** types of molecule labelled **X** and **Y** on **Figure 8**.

X: ....

Y: ....
[2 marks]

The bases in the two strands that make up a DNA molecule always pair up in the same way. **A** always pairs with **T**. **G** always pairs with **C**.

6.3 A section of DNA was analysed.
24% of its nucleotides were found to contain base **A**.

Calculate the percentage of nucleotides in this section of DNA that you would expect to contain base **C**.

Nucleotides that contain base C = ...%
[3 marks]

Question 6 continues on the next page

Turn over ▶

A mutation is a random change in an organism's DNA.

Figure 9 shows the normal order of bases in a section of DNA and then the same section of DNA after a mutation has occurred.

Figure 9

DNA before mutation: T A C T T T A C C
DNA after mutation: T A C T T A A C C

Table 2 shows four DNA base sequences along with the amino acid that each sequence codes for.

Table 2

DNA base sequence	Amino acid coded for
TTA	asparagine
ACC	tryptophan
TTT	lysine
TAC	methionine

6.4 Using the information in **Table 2** and **Figure 9**, write down the order of amino acids coded for **after** the mutation has taken place.

....

....
[1 mark]

6.5 The section of DNA in **Figure 9** codes for part of a protein.
Explain why the mutation shown in **Figure 9** alters the protein that is produced.

....

....
[1 mark]

The genome of an organism is the entire genetic material of that organism. Scientists have now worked out the majority of the human genome.

6.6 Explain how knowledge of the human genome can help scientists trace the migration of certain populations around the world.

....

....

....

....

....

....

[4 marks]

Turn over for the next question

Turn over ▶

7 Plant shoots bend towards the light.

A student wanted to find out if there is a relationship between light intensity and the amount a seedling bends towards the light. She set up the following experiment:

1. Label 5 Petri dishes **A**, **B**, **C** and **D**.
2. Place a layer of moist cotton wool in each Petri dish.
3. Place one cress seed in the centre of each Petri dish.
4. Wait until the seeds have germinated and the plant shoots are 3 cm tall.
5. Position Petri dish **A** 20 cm away from a lamp. Leave for 48 hours.
6. Measure the angle at which the cress seedling bends from a vertical position. Do this using a protractor that measures in 10° intervals.
7. Repeat for the remaining Petri dishes, changing the brightness of the bulb in the lamp each time.

Figure 10 shows the set-up of the apparatus.

Figure 10

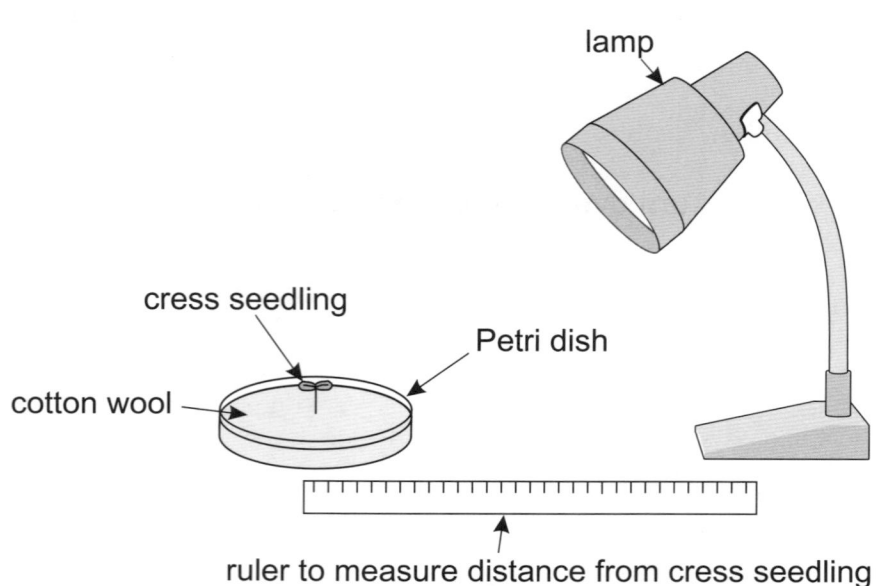

Figure 11 shows how the angle at which each seedling bent was measured.

Figure 11

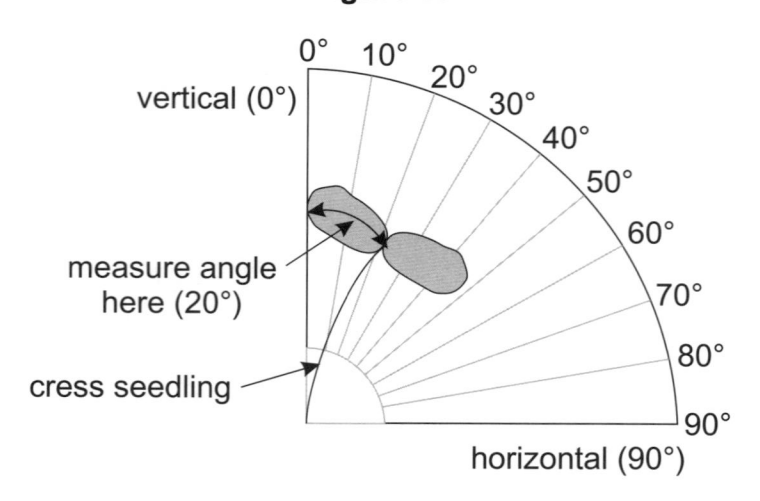

Table 3 shows the results.

Table 3

Petri dish	Brightness of bulb (lumens)	Angle at which seedling bent (°)
A	1125	20
B	900	30
C	600	50
D	375	60

7.1 Suggest **one** way in which the method could be improved to make sure the test gives a more accurate result.

....

....
[1 mark]

7.2 Suggest **one** way in which the method could be improved to make sure the test gives a valid result.

....

....
[1 mark]

7.3 Give **one** conclusion that can be drawn from the results in **Table 3** about the effect of light intensity on the amount a seedling bends.

....

....
[1 mark]

Question 7 continues on the next page

Turn over ▶

Auxin is a hormone that controls the growth of a plant in response to light.

7.4 Explain how auxin causes the seedlings to bend towards the light.

....

....

....

....

....
[3 marks]

7.5 Describe how auxin affects growth in a plant's root cells.

....
[1 mark]

A tropism is growth by plants in response to a stimulus.
Tropisms are positive when part of the plant grows towards a stimulus.
They are negative when part of the plant grows away from a stimulus.

7.6 Name **one** part of a plant that shows positive tropism in response to gravity.
Explain an advantage of this positive tropism to the plant.

Part of plant: ....

Advantage: ....

....

....
[3 marks]

8 The menstrual cycle is controlled by several reproductive hormones.
One of these hormones is LH.

8.1 Describe the role of LH in the menstrual cycle.

....

....
[1 mark]

8.2 LH is produced by the pituitary gland in the brain.
Explain why the pituitary gland is also known as the 'master gland'.

....

....

....
[2 marks]

Question 8 continues on the next page

Figure 12 shows the levels of four different hormones during a 28 day menstrual cycle. It also shows the changes that take place in the thickness of the uterus lining.

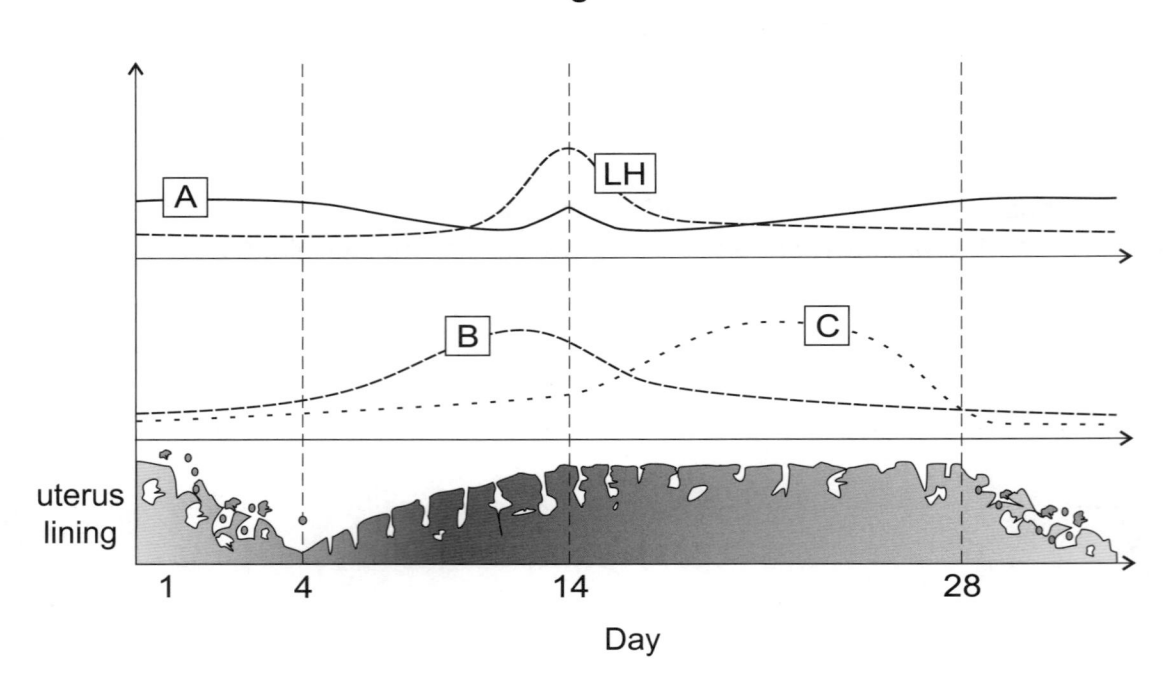

Figure 12

8.3 Name the hormone represented by line **B** in **Figure 12**.
Explain your answer.

Hormone: ....

Explanation: ....

....

....
[3 marks]

8.4 Suggest why, if a fertilised egg implants in the uterus wall, the level of hormone **C** remains high and does not decrease.

....

....

....
[3 marks]

9 The conditions inside the human body are kept relatively steady by various processes. The maintenance of steady internal conditions is called homeostasis.

9.1 Why is it important that the body's internal environment is kept constant?

....

....
[1 mark]

The internal temperature of the body is controlled by homeostasis.

9.2 Explain how the body responds when the temperature of the blood increases.

....

....

....

....

....

....
[4 marks]

Question 9 continues on the next page

The body constantly balances the amount water that enters it against the amount of water that leaves it.

9.3 On a hot day, a person's blood may become more concentrated than normal due to increased water loss by sweating.

Receptors in the brain detect when the blood water content becomes too low.

Explain the sequence of events that occur in the body to return the water content of the blood back to normal once this change has been detected.

....

....

....

....

[3 marks]

10 Guinea pigs can have rough or smooth hair.

The gene that controls hair type has two alleles. Rough hair is controlled by the allele 'R' and smooth hair is controlled by the allele 'r'.

Figure 13 shows a genetic cross between two rough-haired guinea pigs.

Figure 13

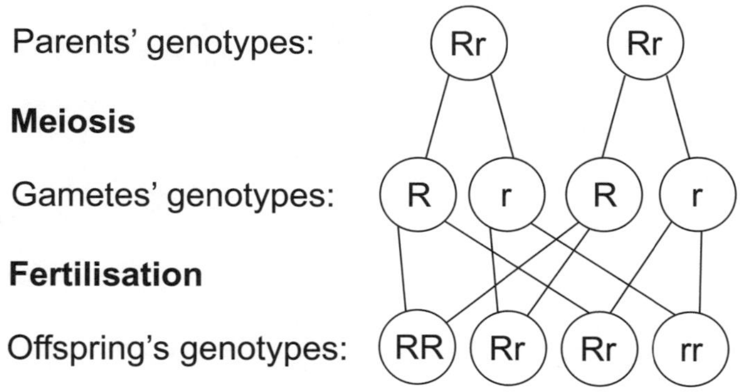

Parents' genotypes:
Rr
Rr
Meiosis
Gametes' genotypes:
R
r
R
r
Fertilisation
Offspring's genotypes:
RR
Rr
Rr
rr

10.1 Use **Figure 13** to explain what happens to the number of chromosomes during meiosis and fertilisation.

[4 marks]

10.2 What is the expected ratio of rough-haired guinea pigs to smooth-haired guinea pigs in the offspring of the cross shown in **Figure 13**?

[1 mark]

Question 10 continues on the next page

Turn over ▶

Leave blank

A heterozygous female guinea pig was crossed with a male guinea pig homozygous for smooth hair. They had a litter of 6 offspring.

10.3 Calculate the number of offspring you would expect to have smooth hair. Draw a Punnett square to explain your answer.

Expected number of offspring with smooth hair: ....
[5 marks]

END OF QUESTIONS

GCSE Biology

Set B Paper 1

Higher Tier

In addition to this paper you should have:
- A ruler.
- A calculator.

Centre name	
Centre number	
Candidate number	

Surname	
Other names	
Candidate signature	

Time allowed:
- 1 hour 45 minutes

Instructions to candidates
- Write your name and other details in the spaces provided above.
- Answer **all** questions in the spaces provided.
- Do all rough work on the paper.
- Cross out any work you do not want to be marked.

Information for candidates
- The marks available are given in brackets at the end of each question.
- There are 100 marks available for this paper.
- You are allowed to use a calculator.
- You should use good English and present your answers in a clear and organised way.
- For Questions 3.4, 5.4 and 7.1 ensure that your answers have a clear and logical structure, include the right scientific terms, spelt correctly and include detailed, relevant information.

Advice to candidates
- In calculations show clearly how you worked out your answers.

Answer **all** questions in the spaces provided

1 In plants, stem cells are found in regions called meristems.

1.1 Give **two** sites in a plant where meristem tissue is found.

1. ....

2. ....
[2 marks]

1.2 Describe the difference between stem cells in mature plants and stem cells in adult humans.

....

....

....
[2 marks]

1.3 Give **one** site where adult stem cells are found in humans.

....
[1 mark]

Scientists can create new plants by isolating meristem tissue and cloning it.

1.4 Name the type of plant cell division that produces clones.

....
[1 mark]

1.5 Give **two** benefits of producing plants through cloning, rather than letting them reproduce naturally.

1. ....

2. ....
[2 marks]

2 **Figure 1** shows some of the organs in the human digestive system.

Figure 1

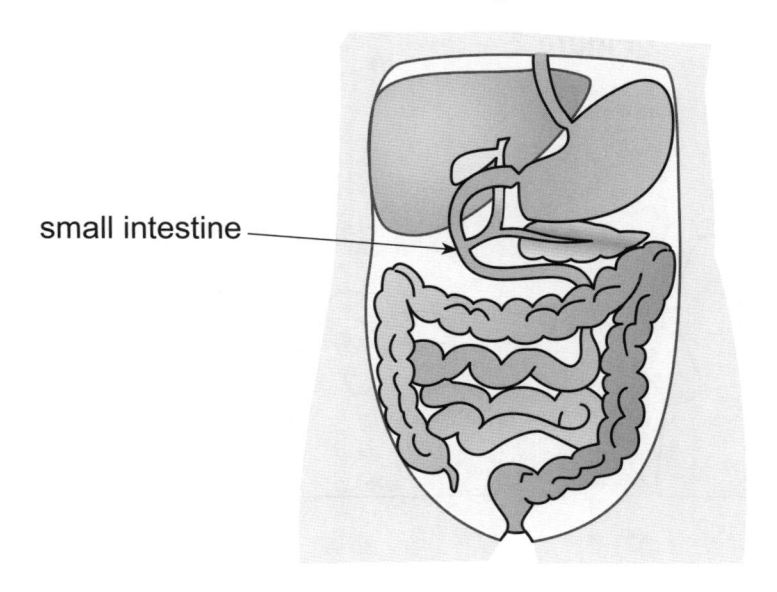

small intestine

Bile plays an important role in the digestion of fats.

2.1 Bile is produced by the liver and stored in the gall bladder.
Label the **liver** and the **gall bladder** on **Figure 1**.

[2 marks]

2.2 Give **two** different functions of bile.
Explain the importance of each function you have given.

Function: ....

Explanation: ....

....

Function: ....

Explanation: ....

....

[4 marks]

Question 2 continues on the next page

Turn over ▶

In a healthy person, the small intestine is lined with millions of villi.

Figure 2 shows healthy villi and villi that have been damaged by a digestive disease.

Figure 2

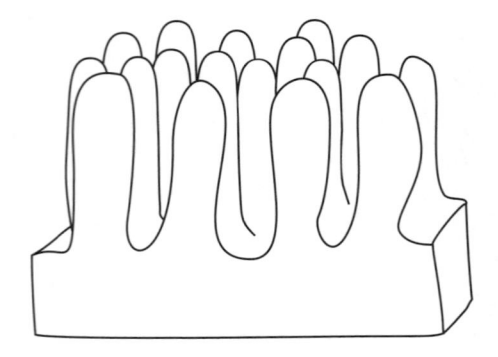

healthy villi

damaged villi

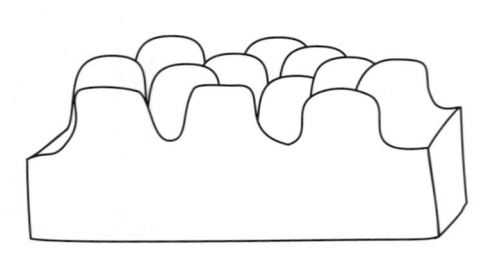

2.3 Explain why digested food molecules are absorbed more slowly across the damaged villi than the healthy villi.

....

....

....

....
[3 marks]

3   The leaves of a plant can be affected by fungal diseases.

3.1 Name **one** fungal disease that affects plant leaves.
     Explain why the disease reduces plant growth.

     Disease: ....

     Explanation: ....

     ....
     [3 marks]

     A gardener discovers that a plant in his garden is infected with a fungal disease.

3.2 Explain why replanting the affected plant a few metres further away from the other plants in his garden may **not** help to prevent the spread of the disease.

     ....

     ....
     [1 mark]

3.3 Suggest **one** method the gardener could use to get rid of the fungal disease.

     ....
     [1 mark]

Question 3 continues on the next page

Figure 3 shows a diagram of a leaf.

Leave blank

Figure 3

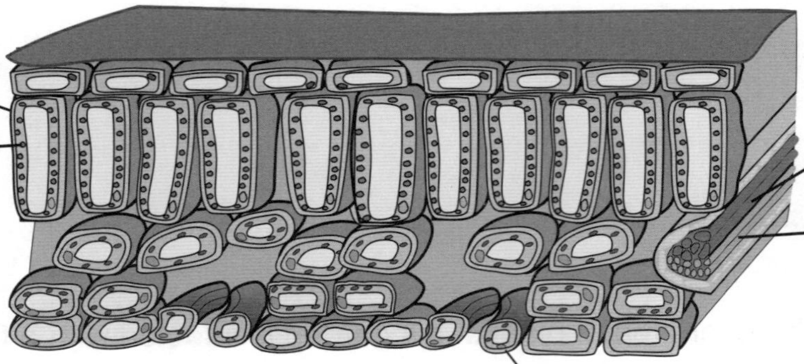
palisade leaf cell
chloroplast
xylem
phloem
guard cell

3.4 Use **Figure 3** and your own knowledge to explain how the tissues in a leaf are adapted for photosynthesis.

....

....

....

....

....

....

....

....

....

....

....

[6 marks]

4 Respiration in cells can take place aerobically or anaerobically to transfer energy.

4.1 Which of the following statements about **aerobic** respiration is correct?
Tick **one** box.

☐ Aerobic respiration uses oxygen and produces ethanol and carbon dioxide.

☐ Aerobic respiration does not use oxygen and produces carbon dioxide and water.

☐ Aerobic respiration uses oxygen and produces carbon dioxide and water.

☐ Aerobic respiration does not use oxygen and produces ethanol and carbon dioxide.

[1 mark]

4.2 Energy transferred by respiration is used in metabolism.
Explain what is meant by the term **metabolism**.

....

....
[1 mark]

Question 4 continues on the next page

Turn over ▶

A student decided to investigate how respiring seeds affect the temperature of their surroundings.

Figure 4 shows how the student set up her experiment.

Figure 4

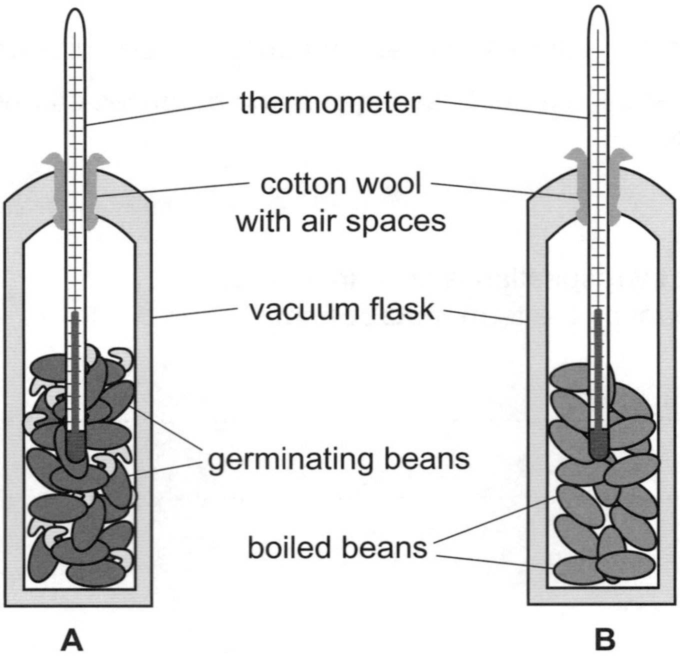

thermometer
cotton wool
with air spaces
vacuum flask
germinating beans
boiled beans
A
B

The temperature inside the flasks was recorded on day 1 of the experiment, immediately after the beans had been added to the flasks.

The temperature inside the flasks was then recorded every day at the same time for another 4 days.

Table 1 shows the results of the experiment.

Table 1

	Temperature (°C)	
Day	**Flask A**	**Flask B**
1	18	18
2	20	19
3	21	18
4	24	19
5	26	19

Leave blank

4.3 Describe the overall trend in results shown in **Table 1** for **Flask A**.

....

....
[1 mark]

4.4 Suggest an explanation for the **Flask A** results.

....

....

....
[2 marks]

4.5 Suggest why boiled beans were used in **Flask B** in the experiment.

....

....

....

....
[3 marks]

Turn over for the next question

Turn over ▶

5 The heart pumps blood around the body through a network of blood vessels. **Figure 5** shows a diagram of the heart.

Figure 5

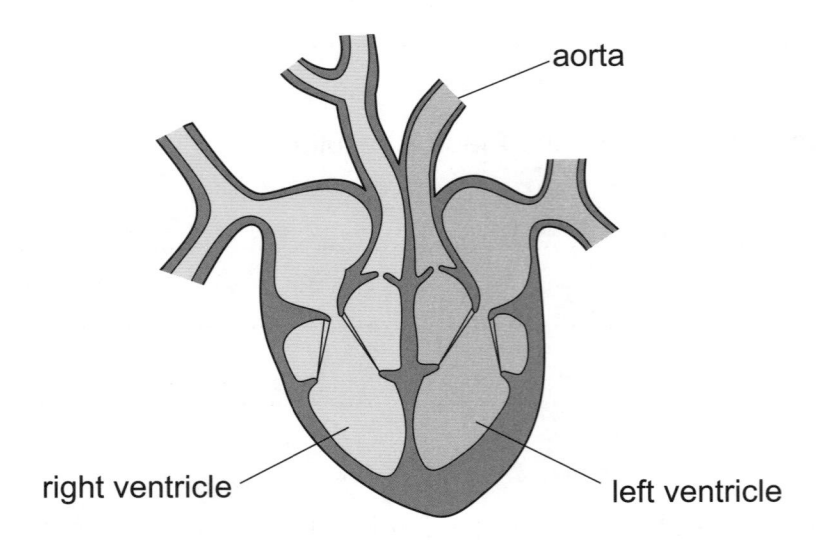

5.1 On **Figure 5**, label with the letter **A** the chamber of the heart where the pacemaker cells are located.

[1 mark]

5.2 **Figure 5** shows that the left ventricle wall is thicker than the right ventricle wall. Suggest an explanation for this.

....

....

....

[3 marks]

5.3 A scientist estimates that in 7 minutes, 32 750 cm³ of blood is pumped through an individual's aorta.
Calculate the rate of blood flow through the individual's aorta in dm³/min.
Give your answer to 2 significant figures.

Rate of blood flow: .... dm³/min

[3 marks]

5.4 Use **Figure 5** and your own knowledge to describe how blood flows through the right and left sides of the heart.

....

....

....

....

....

....

....

....

....

....

....

[6 marks]

Sometimes a person's heart does not beat regularly.

5.5 Give **one** treatment for an irregular heartbeat.
Explain how this treatment would help to correct the irregular heartbeat.

Treatment: ....

Explanation: ....

....

[2 marks]

Turn over for the next question

Turn over ▶

6 Table 2 shows the dimensions of three cubes, **A**, **B** and **C**. Each cube represents a different single-celled organism that lives in a freshwater pond.
The cubes are not drawn to scale.

Table 2

	A	B	C
Cube dimensions (mm)	0.5 × 0.5 × 0.5	0.1 × 0.1 × 0.1	0.3 × 0.3 × 0.3
Surface area (mm²)	X	0.06	0.54
Volume (mm³)	0.125	Y	0.027
Surface area : volume	12:1	60:1	Z

6.1 Calculate the values of **X**, **Y** and **Z** in Table 2.

X = ... mm²

Y = ... mm³

Z = ... : 1

[3 marks]

6.2 How many times bigger is the surface area to volume ratio of cube **B** than that of cube **A**?

....

[1 mark]

The organisms represented by the cubes in **Table 2** all need to exchange substances with their environment.

6.3 Which cube (**A**, **B** or **C**) represents the organism with the slowest rate of exchange? Explain your answer.

Cube: ....

Explanation: ....

....
[2 marks]

6.4 Explain how the temperature of the pond water could affect the rate at which the organisms exchange substances with their environment.

....

....

....
[2 marks]

Turn over for the next question

7 A student investigated the effect of different concentrations of salt solution on potato tissue.

The student's results are shown in **Table 3**.

Table 3

	Concentration of salt solution (mol/dm³)				
	0	0.1	0.3	0.5	0.7
initial mass of potato (g)	34.2	32.0	37.0	32.9	35.0
final mass of potato (g)	36.1	33.4	36.3	32.1	X
% change in mass	5.56	4.38	− 1.89	− 2.43	− 4.00

7.1 Describe a method that the student could have used to obtain his results. Include a description of the variables that the student should have controlled.

....

....

....

....

....

....

....

....

[4 marks]

7.2 Calculate the value of **X** in **Table 3**.

final mass = ... g

[2 marks]

7.3 When potato tissue is placed in a fluid with the same concentration as the fluid inside its cells, there is no overall change in mass. Explain why.

....

....
[1 mark]

7.4 Explain how the student could determine the concentration of the fluid inside the potato experimentally.

....

....

....
[2 marks]

7.5 The student made the following hypothesis before conducting the experiment:
'Immersing potato tissue in salt solution results in the potato tissue losing mass.'

Use the results in **Table 3** to explain whether or not the student's hypothesis was confirmed.

....

....
[1 mark]

7.6 Garden weeds can be killed by spraying them with a concentrated salt solution.
Suggest how the concentrated salt solution kills the weeds.
Explain your answer.

....

....

....

....
[2 marks]

Turn over for the next question

Turn over ▶

8 Photosynthesis is a reaction which occurs in the leaves of a plant.

Leave blank

8.1 Photosynthesis is described as an endothermic reaction.
Explain what this means.

....

....

[1 mark]

The rate of photosynthesis has several limiting factors.

Figure 6 shows the effect of light intensity on the rate of photosynthesis.

Figure 6

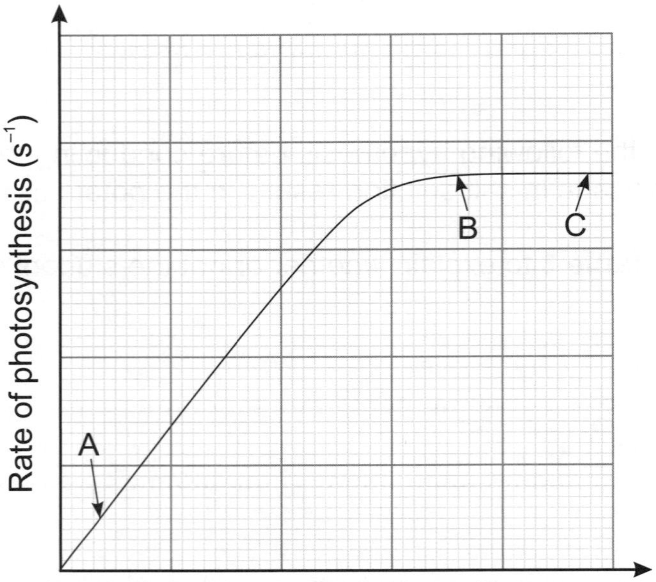

8.2 Between which two points in **Figure 6** is light intensity the limiting factor on the rate of photosynthesis?
Tick **one** box.

☐ **A** and **B** ☐ **B** and **C** ☐ **A** and **C**

[1 mark]

Figure 7 shows the effect of light intensity and carbon dioxide on the rate of photosynthesis.

Leave blank

Figure 7

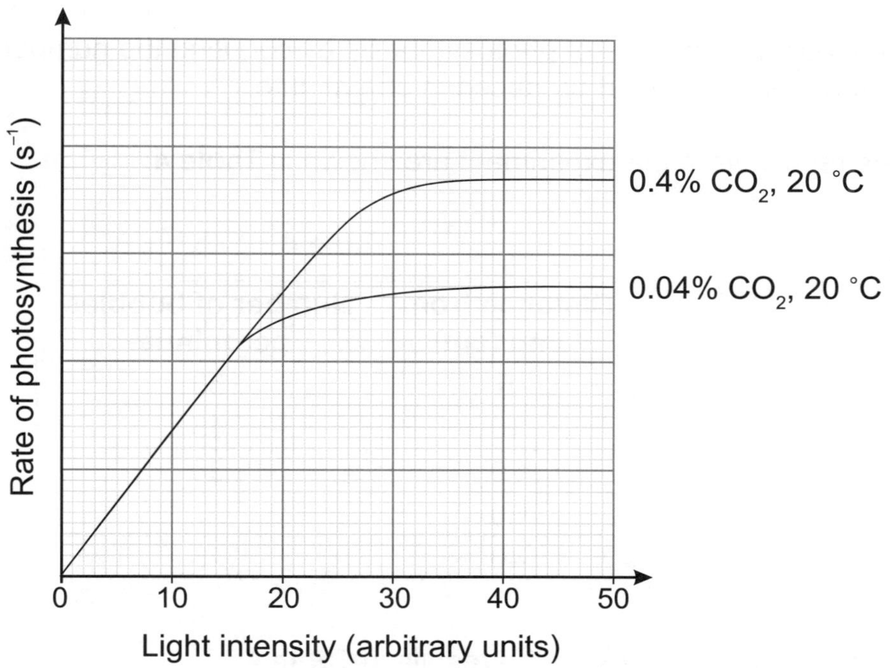

Rate of photosynthesis (s⁻¹)
0.4% CO₂, 20 °C
0.04% CO₂, 20 °C
0
10
20
30
40
50
Light intensity (arbitrary units)

8.3 A student looks at **Figure 7** and says:
'At a light intensity of 30 units and a carbon dioxide concentration of 0.04%, carbon dioxide concentration is the limiting factor for photosynthesis.'

Describe the evidence from **Figure 7** which supports this statement.

....

....

....

....

[2 marks]

Question 8 continues on the next page

Turn over ▶

A student investigated the effect of light intensity on the rate of photosynthesis in pondweed.

He varied the light intensity by changing the distance of the pondweed from a lamp.

He measured the rate of photosynthesis by counting the number of bubbles of oxygen the pondweed produced in one minute.

The results from the experiment are shown in **Table 4**.

Table 4

Distance from lamp (cm)	Number of bubbles per minute
5	53
10	45
20	34
30	27
40	23

8.4 Complete **Figure 8** using the results in **Table 4**.

- Complete the *x*-axis. Include a label and a suitable scale.
- Plot the number of bubbles per minute for each distance.
- Draw a curve of best fit.

Figure 8

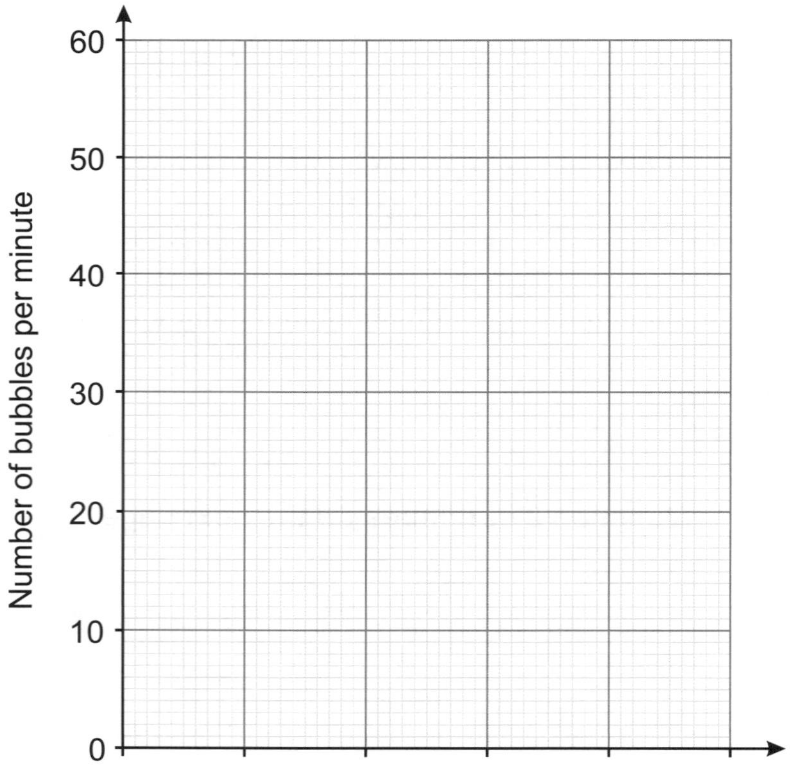

[3 marks]

8.5 Use the graph in **Figure 8** to estimate the distance the lamp would have to be from the beaker for 32 bubbles per minute to have been produced.

Distance = ... cm
[1 mark]

The relationship between light intensity and distance from the plant is governed by the inverse square law.

8.6 Calculate the light intensity when the lamp is 40 cm away from the pondweed. Use the formula:

$$\text{light intensity} = \frac{1}{\text{distance}^2}$$

Give your answer in standard form.

light intensity = ... arbitrary units
[2 marks]

Turn over for the next question

9 Plants require mineral ions for healthy growth.
They absorb these ions from the soil into their root hairs.

Mineral ions are present in low concentrations in the soil.
They are absorbed into root hair cells by active transport.

9.1 Use the information above to explain why root hair cells contain many mitochondria.

....

....

....
[2 marks]

Plants can be damaged by mineral ion deficiencies.

A student set up an experiment to determine the effect of mineral ion deficiencies on the growth of plants.

She took two seedlings and placed each one into a test tube.
This is shown in **Figure 9**.

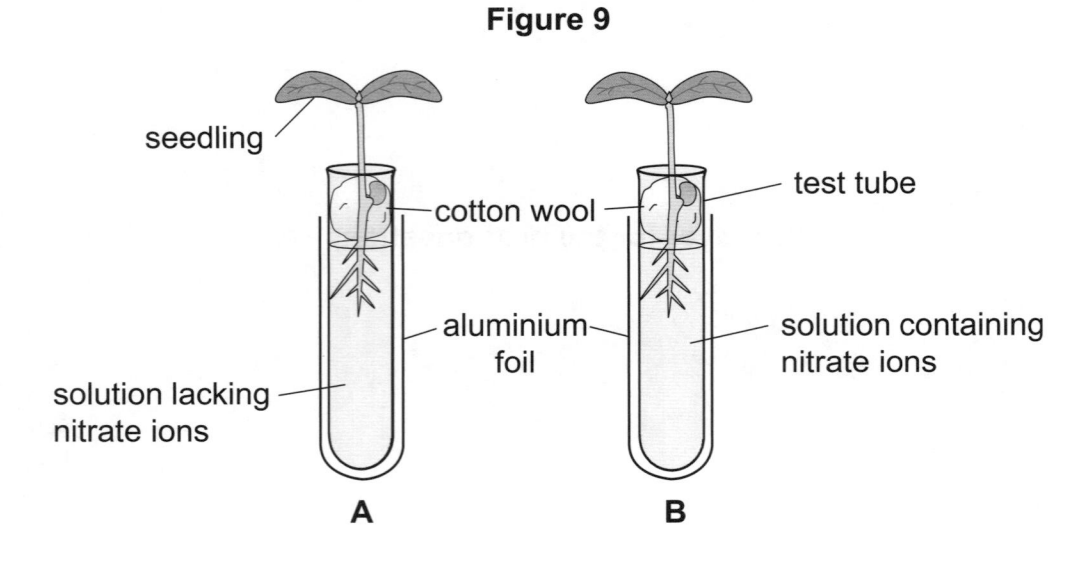

Figure 9

The test tubes were wrapped in a layer of aluminium foil to exclude light and to prevent algae from growing in the solution.

The seedlings were left to grow in these solutions for four weeks, during which time the level of water in the test tubes was kept topped up with distilled water.

After four weeks the condition of the plants was recorded.

9.2 Suggest why it was important to stop algae growing in the solutions.

....

....

....
[2 marks]

9.3 Suggest **one** difference you would expect to see between the seedlings in test tubes **A** and **B** after four weeks. Explain your answer.

Difference: ....

....

Explanation: ....

....
[3 marks]

9.4 After two weeks, the seedlings in both test tubes **A** and **B** showed signs of chlorosis. Suggest why.

....

....
[1 mark]

Turn over for the next question

10 A group of students carried out an experiment to determine the effect of temperature on the ability of biological washing powder to remove a stain from clothing.

Biological washing powder contains one or more enzymes.

The students used egg yolk as the stain.

This is the method they used:

1. Cut pieces of cloth into 20 cm² pieces.
2. Apply egg yolk to the cloth so that it covers an area of 9 cm². Leave to dry.
3. Dissolve biological washing powder in a beaker of warm water at 20 °C.
4. Place one piece of the stained cloth into the beaker. Stir.
5. Soak for 20 minutes.
6. Remove the cloth from the beaker and allow to dry.
7. Rate the colour of the stain on a scale from 1 to 10. 1 indicates no change from the original stain. 10 is completely clean.
8. Repeat steps 1-7 for temperatures of 40 °C, 60 °C and 80 °C.

The results are shown in **Table 5**.

Table 5

Temperature (°C)	Rating given to stain after washing (scale of 1 to 10)
20	3
40	9
60	7
80	2

Egg yolk is rich in proteins and lipids.

10.1 Name **two** types of enzyme which would need to be present in the biological washing powder to remove the egg yolk stain.

1. ....

2. ....
[2 marks]

The students made the following conclusion from their results:

'The optimum temperature for this biological washing powder must be 40°C, as the colour change of the stain was greatest at this temperature.'

10.2 Explain why the students may be wrong in the conclusion they have made.

....

....

....
[2 marks]

10.3 Suggest why there was very little colour change in the stain at 80°C.

....

....

....

....
[3 marks]

10.4 Suggest **two** possible sources of error in the students' method.

1. ....

....

2. ....

....
[2 marks]

10.5 The pH of the washing powder solution in which the cloth was soaked started off at pH 10.
Suggest what would happen to the pH of the water in which the cloth was soaked. Explain your answer.

....

....

....
[2 marks]

END OF QUESTIONS

GCSE Biology

Set B Paper 2

Higher Tier

In addition to this paper you should have:
- A ruler.
- A calculator.

Centre name

Centre number

Candidate number

Surname

Other names

Candidate signature

Time allowed:
- 1 hour 45 minutes

Instructions to candidates
- Write your name and other details in the spaces provided above.
- Answer **all** questions in the spaces provided.
- Do all rough work on the paper.
- Cross out any work you do not want to be marked.

Information for candidates
- The marks available are given in brackets at the end of each question.
- There are 100 marks available for this paper.
- You are allowed to use a calculator.
- You should use good English and present your answers in a clear and organised way.
- For Questions 5.4, 7.4 and 9.1 ensure that your answers have a clear and logical structure, include the right scientific terms, spelt correctly and include detailed, relevant information.

Advice to candidates
- In calculations show clearly how you worked out your answers.

Answer **all** questions in the spaces provided

1 Classification is a process that scientists use to put organisms into groups.

1.1 When classifying organisms, what is the correct order for the groups from largest to smallest? Tick **one** box.

☐ kingdom, phylum, class, order, family, genus, species

☐ phylum, family, kingdom, order, class, genus, species

☐ kingdom, phylum, family, order, class, species, genus

☐ kingdom, class, phylum, order, family, species, genus

[1 mark]

Classification methods have changed over time.

Traditional classification methods grouped organisms according to their structure and characteristics.

1.2 Name the scientist that developed the traditional classification method.

....
[1 mark]

In the 1990's, a classification method called the 'three-domain system' was developed. In this system, organisms are first divided into three domains.

Table 1 shows some of the characteristics of two of these domains.

Table 1

Domain	Characteristics
X	Cells don't contain a nucleus. First found in extreme environments, such as salt lakes. Originally thought to be primitive bacteria.
Y	Cells usually contain a nucleus, mitochondria and ribosomes.

1.3 Which of the three domains is represented by **X** in **Table 1**?

....
[1 mark]

1.4 Give **one** example of a type of organism belonging to the domain represented by **Y** in **Table 1**.

....
[1 mark]

Scientists use evolutionary trees to show how organisms are related.

1.5 Scientists use current classification data to create evolutionary trees for living organisms.
What information do they use to create evolutionary trees for **extinct** organisms?

....
[1 mark]

Figure 1 shows an evolutionary tree for organisms **A** to **M**.

Figure 1

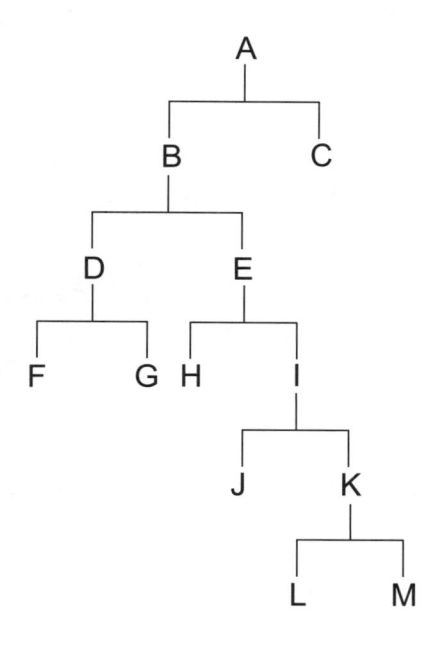

```
            A
           / \
          B   C
         / \
        D   E
       /|   |\
      F G   H I
              |
             / \
            J   K
               / \
              L   M
```

1.6 Which species is the most recent common ancestor of species **G** and **J**?

Species: ....
[1 mark]

1.7 Which pair of species, **G and H** or **L and M**, are more closely related?
Explain your answer.

Pair of species: ....

Explanation: ....

....
[1 mark]

Turn over for the next question

Turn over ▶

2 Figure 2 shows a diagram of a woodland ecosystem and some of the animals and plants within it.

Figure 2

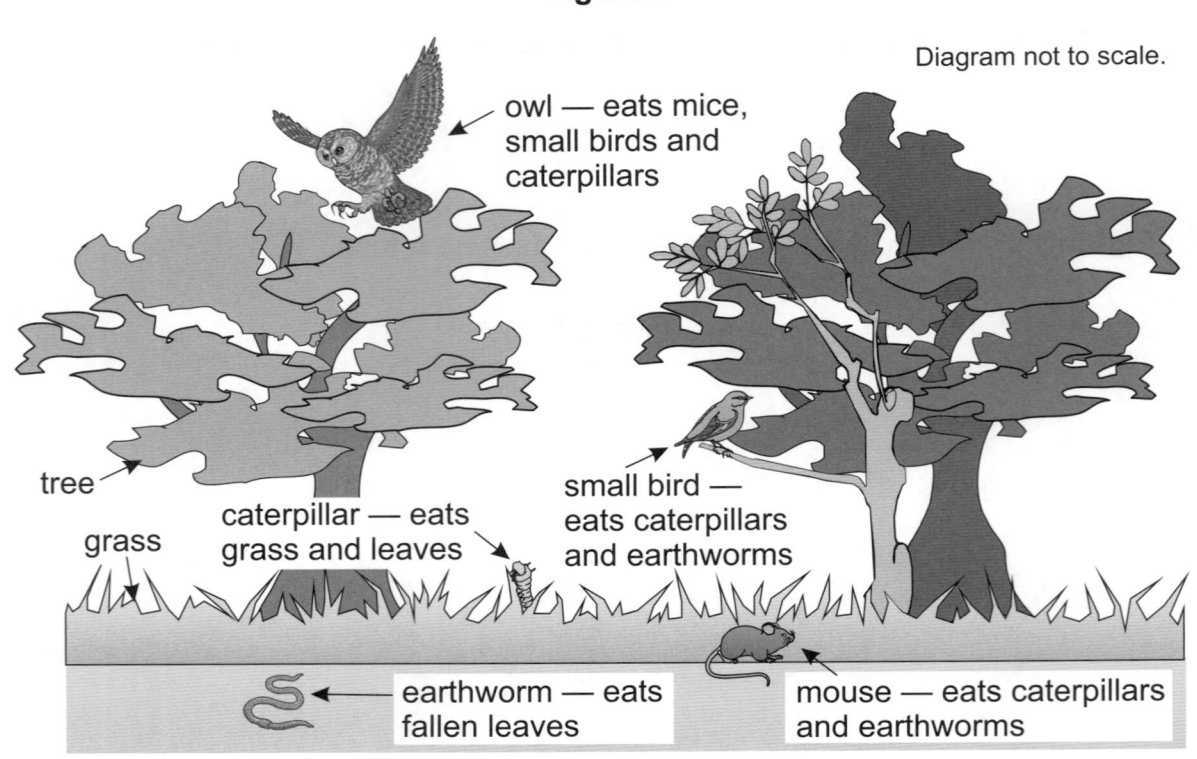

Diagram not to scale.

owl — eats mice, small birds and caterpillars

tree

grass

caterpillar — eats grass and leaves

small bird — eats caterpillars and earthworms

earthworm — eats fallen leaves

mouse — eats caterpillars and earthworms

2.1 Suggest **two** abiotic factors that the trees and grass in **Figure 2** compete for.

1. ....

2. ....
[2 marks]

2.2 Suggest **two** biotic factors that the animals shown in **Figure 2** compete for.

1. ....

2. ....
[2 marks]

2.3 Using information in **Figure 2**, write down a food chain consisting of **four** trophic levels.

....

....
[2 marks]

2.4 Which organism in **Figure 2** is an apex predator?

....
[1 mark]

2.5 Suggest **two** adaptations of the organism you named in **2.4** that enable it to be a successful predator. Give a reason why each adaptation is beneficial.

Adaptation 1: ....

Reason: ....

Adaptation 2: ....

Reason: ....
[2 marks]

Question 2 continues on the next page

Biomass is the mass of organisms at each trophic level in a food chain. Only about 10% of the biomass from each trophic level is transferred to the next level.

2.6 Explain why not all of the biomass in the food that an organism eats is transferred to the next trophic level.

....

....

....
[2 marks]

Table 2 shows the amount of biomass available at each trophic level in a woodland food chain.

Table 2

Trophic level	1	2	3	4
Biomass available (arbitrary units)	53.5	5.54	0.50	0.05
Efficiency of biomass transfer (%)	—	10.4	X	10.0

2.7 Calculate the value of **X** in Table 2.
Use the equation:

$$\text{Efficiency} = \frac{\text{biomass transferred to next level}}{\text{biomass available at the previous level}} \times 100$$

Give your answer to **3** significant figures.

X = ...%
[2 marks]

3 Humans can use techniques such as selective breeding and genetic engineering to produce organisms with desired characteristics.

Many different types of fruit are produced by selective breeding.

A farmer grows several different varieties of raspberry plant on her farm.

Table 3 shows some of the characteristics of these raspberry plants.
Each characteristic is partly controlled by the plants' genes.

Table 3

Raspberry Plant Variety	Fruit Characteristics				
	Size	Firmness	Taste	Shelf-life	Yield
A	Large	Soft	Sour	Short	High
B	Medium	Hard	Sweet	Short	Low
C	Small	Hard	Sweet	Long	Medium

The farmer would like to produce a plant that has these characteristics:

- Large fruit
- Soft fruit
- Sweet taste
- Long shelf-life
- High yield

3.1 Suggest which **two** raspberry plant varieties from **Table 3** should be bred together to produce the desired characteristics.

....
[1 mark]

3.2 Describe how the farmer would use the selected raspberry plants to produce plants with the desired characteristics.

....

....

....

....

....
[3 marks]

Question 3 continues on the next page

Turn over ▶

3.3 The farmer notices that a small number of her selectively-bred raspberry plants have started to die from a disease.
Explain why she might be concerned that the disease will dramatically reduce the population size of her raspberry plants.

....

....

....
[2 marks]

Crop plants with desirable characteristics can also be produced by genetic engineering.

For example, 'golden rice' is a genetically engineered crop.

It was created to have characteristics that may be beneficial for people who live in developing countries.

3.4 Give **one** way in which 'golden rice' may help to improve the health of people living in developing countries.

....

....
[1 mark]

Genetic engineering is also useful in medicine.

3.5 Describe how genetic engineering is involved in the treatment of Type 1 diabetes.

....

....

....
[2 marks]

4 An optician suspected that one of his patients had a bacterial infection in his eye. He shone a bright light into the eye to take a closer look.

The patient's pupil became smaller in response to the bright light.
This is the opposite response to that of the pupil in dim light conditions.

4.1 Suggest the changes that occurred in the patient's eye to cause the pupil to become smaller.

....

....

....
[2 marks]

The reaction that occurred in the patient's eye was a reflex action.

4.2 Suggest why it is helpful for the body to have a reflex action in response to bright light.

....

....
[1 mark]

4.3 What is the correct sequence of events that brought about the reflex action in the patient's eye?
Tick **one** box.

☐ stimulus → coordinator → receptor → effector → response

☐ receptor → stimulus → effector → coordinator → response

☐ stimulus → receptor → effector → coordinator → response

☐ stimulus → receptor → coordinator → effector → response

[1 mark]

Question 4 continues on the next page

Turn over ▶

The patient was prescribed a course of antibiotic eye drops to treat his infection.

4.4 Explain why it was important for the patient to complete the full course of eye drops.

....

....

....
[3 marks]

Once his infection had cleared up, the patient visited the optician again for a sight test. The patient reported that his vision had gradually become blurred in the last year.

Figure 3 shows how light rays enter one of the patient's eyes.

Figure 3

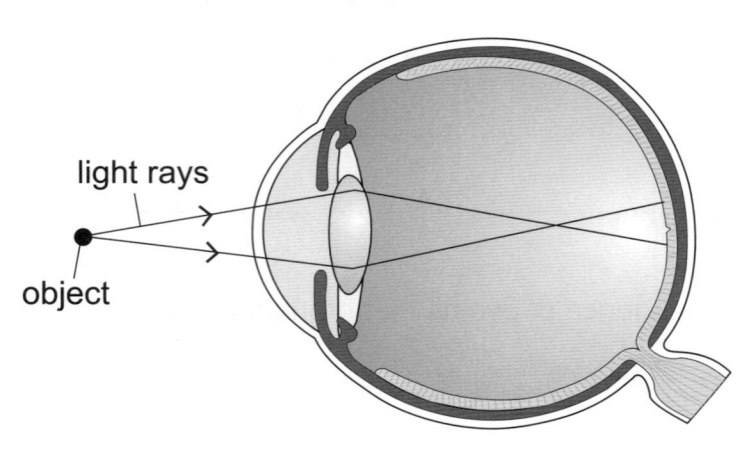

4.5 Name the vision defect shown in **Figure 3**.

....
[1 mark]

4.6 Using **Figure 3**, give **one** reason why the patient's vision is blurred.

....

....
[1 mark]

Figure 4 shows three different shaped lenses.

Figure 4

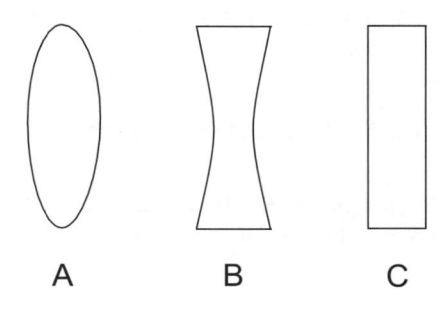

A   B   C

4.7 Explain how a spectacle lens can correct a person's vision.

....

....

....
[2 marks]

4.8 Which lens in **Figure 4** (**A**, **B** or **C**) would correct the patient's blurred vision?

....
[1 mark]

4.9 The patient didn't want to correct his vision by wearing spectacles.

Give **one** other method the patient could use to correct his vision.

....
[1 mark]

Turn over for the next question

5 A group of students are planning to carry out an experiment to investigate how listening to music at different volumes affects reaction time.

They plan to measure reaction time by measuring the distance a ruler drops before it is caught.

The students have recruited three volunteers to take part in their experiment.

Before they begin their investigation, the students test the reaction time of each volunteer when they are not listening to music.

Table 4 shows the results.

Table 4

Repeat	Distance ruler dropped (cm)		
	Volunteer 1	Volunteer 2	Volunteer 3
1	17	10	16
2	17	9	14
3	15	11	13
4	16	11	14
5	16	9	14
6	15	10	13
Mean	X	10	14

5.1 What is the modal distance the ruler dropped for **Volunteer 3**?

.... cm
[1 mark]

5.2 Calculate the value of **X** in **Table 4**.

X = ... cm
[1 mark]

5.3 Suggest why it is important to measure reaction time when the volunteers are not listening to music.

....

....
[1 mark]

As part of their investigation, the students make the following hypothesis:

'The higher the volume of music being listened to, the slower a person's reaction time will be.'

They are planning to use the following equipment in their investigation:
- mp3 player
- headphones
- 30 cm ruler

5.4 Suggest a method the students could use to investigate their hypothesis. Include details about steps they should take to get valid results.

....

....

....

....

....

....

....

....

....

....

....

....

....

[6 marks]

Question 5 continues on the next page

Turn over ▶

Reaction time depends on how quickly nerve impulses are transmitted in the body.

5.5 A nerve in one of the volunteer's arms is 0.5 metres long.
It takes 0.01 seconds for one impulse to travel the length of the nerve.
What is the speed of the impulse?
Tick **one** box.

☐ 0.5 metres/second

☐ 50 metres/second

☐ 0.005 metres/second

☐ 0.02 metres/second

[1 mark]

6 Lipase enzymes break down fat in the small intestine into glycerol and fatty acids.

Milk contains fat.

A group of students investigated the effect of temperature on the rate of decay of milk by lipase.

This is the method they used:

1. Add 1 cm³ of lipase solution to a test tube labelled **A**.
2. Add 5 cm³ of milk, 5 drops of phenolphthalein indicator and 7 cm³ of sodium carbonate solution to a test tube labelled **B**. (The solution in this test tube will be alkaline and pink in colour.)
3. Place both test tubes in a water bath at 10 °C. Leave them to reach the temperature of the water bath.
4. Transfer the lipase solution from test tube **A** into test tube **B**. Stir with a glass rod and start a stop watch immediately.
5. Time how long it takes for the mixture to lose its pink colour and become white.
6. Repeat stages 1-5 at temperatures of 20, 30, and 40 °C.

The students' results are shown in **Table 5**.

Table 5

Temperature (°C)	Time taken for pink colour to disappear (s)	Rate of reaction (s⁻¹)
10	302	3.3
20	266	3.8
30	246	4.1
40		X

6.1 The time taken for the pink colour to disappear at 40 °C was 3 minutes 48 seconds. Use this information to calculate the value of **X** in **Table 5**.
Use the equation:

Rate = $\frac{1000}{time}$

Give your answer to **2** significant figures.

X = ... s⁻¹
[2 marks]

Question 6 continues on the next page

6.2 Complete **Figure 5** using the data from **Table 5** and your answer to **6.1**.

- Plot the rate of reaction for each temperature.
- Draw a curve of best fit.

Leave blank

Figure 5

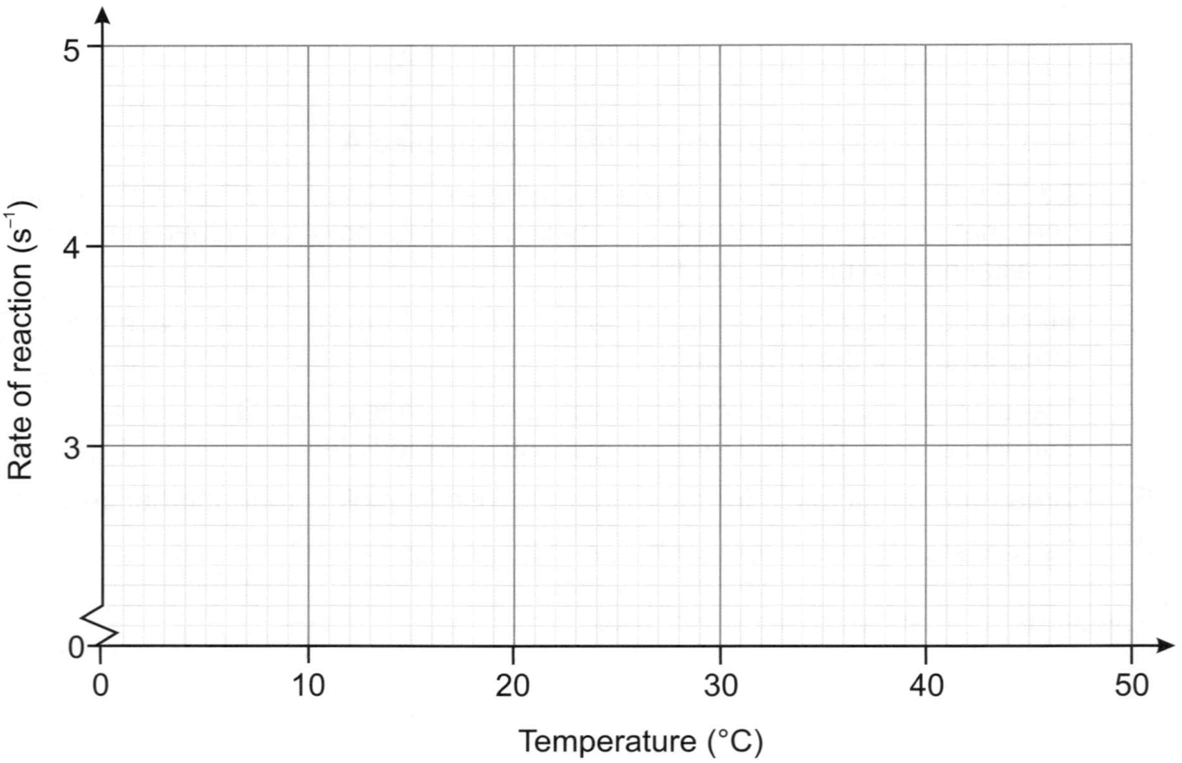

[2 marks]

6.3 Give **one** conclusion that can be drawn from the students' results.

....

....

[1 mark]

Phenolphthalein acts as an indicator dye.
Figure 6 shows how pH affects the colour of phenolphthalein.

Figure 6

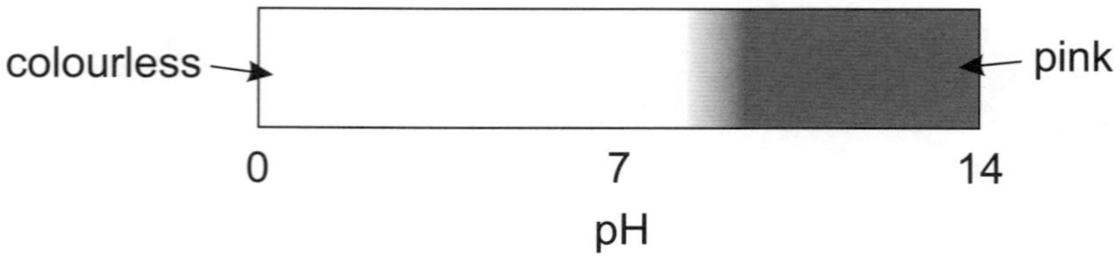

6.4 Use **Figure 6** to explain why the mixture in the experiment loses its pink colour.

....

....

....
[2 marks]

The students used an electric water bath in their experiment.

The thermostat in the water bath could only maintain temperatures above room temperature, which was around 18 °C.

The water in the water bath was at room temperature before the students started their experiment.

6.5 Suggest how the students could have achieved and maintained a temperature of 10 °C in the water bath.

....

....

....

....
[3 marks]

6.6 The students found it very difficult to judge the end point of the reaction.
The end point is when the reaction mixture first loses its pink colour.

Suggest how the students could improve the method to make judging the end point more accurate.

....

....
[1 mark]

Question 6 continues on the next page

Turn over ▶

6.7 Suggest **one** further experiment the students could carry out to be sure that the colour change that occurred during the experiment was due to the activity of the enzyme. Explain your answer.

....

....

....
[2 marks]

The milk used in the experiment was made by mixing milk powder with water.

Milk powder is created by removing the water from regular milk.

6.8 Suggest why milk powder decays more slowly than regular milk.

....

....

....
[2 marks]

Leave blank

7 The kidneys are involved in the excretion of excess amino acids.

7.1 Explain what happens to excess amino acids that are present in the blood so that they can be excreted safely by the kidneys.

....

....

....

....

....

[4 marks]

The kidneys are involved in creating the right balance of ions in the body.

7.2 Explain why having the wrong balance of ions in the blood could have a negative effect on the body.

....

....

....

....

[3 marks]

Kidney failure is when a person's kidneys stop working correctly.
One treatment for kidney failure is dialysis treatment.

Figure 7 shows the operation of a dialysis machine.

Figure 7

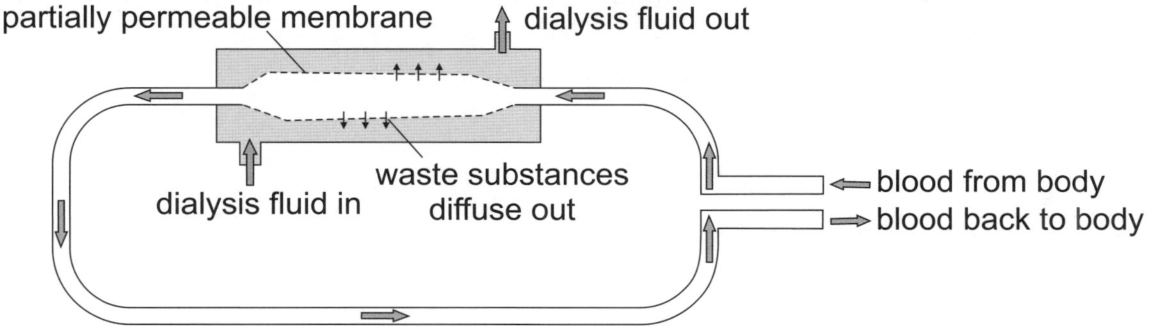

Question 7 continues on the next page

Turn over ▶

Glucose can pass across the partially permeable membrane in a dialysis machine.

7.3 Explain how the dialysis machine ensures that the glucose concentration of blood re-entering the body is the same as the glucose concentration of healthy blood.

....

....

....
[2 marks]

People who have kidney failure may be also be treated by organ transplant.

7.4 Evaluate the use of a dialysis machine and an organ transplant to treat kidney failure. Your answer should include a justified conclusion about which method is most beneficial.

....

....

....

....

....

....

....

....

....

....
[4 marks]

8 Cystic fibrosis is an inherited disorder that affects the cell membranes. It results in thick, sticky mucus building up in some of the body's organs.

The condition is caused by a recessive allele, f.

Figure 8 shows a genetic cross between two parents both with the genotype Ff.

Figure 8

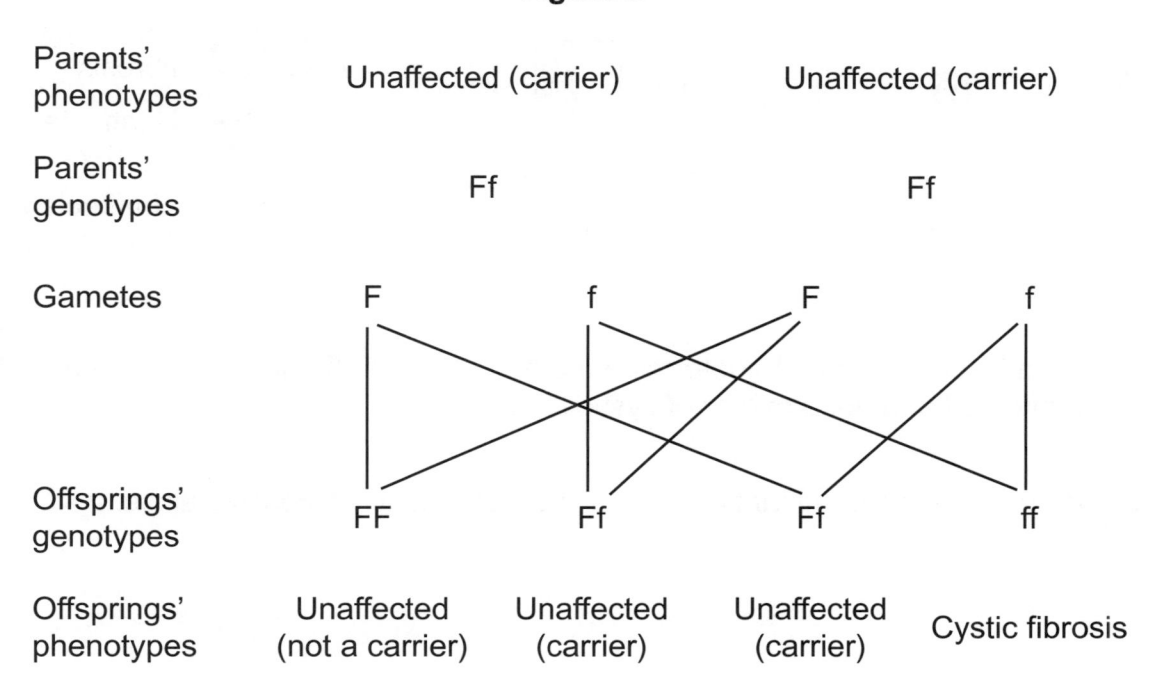

Parents' phenotypes	Unaffected (carrier)	Unaffected (carrier)
Parents' genotypes	Ff	Ff
Gametes	F f	F f
Offsprings' genotypes	FF Ff Ff ff
Offsprings' phenotypes	Unaffected (not a carrier)	Unaffected (carrier)	Unaffected (carrier)	Cystic fibrosis

8.1 On **Figure 8**, write a letter **Y** to show the point at which **fertilisation** takes place.
[1 mark]

8.2 According to **Figure 8**, what is the expected ratio of offspring who are carriers of cystic fibrosis to offspring with cystic fibrosis?

....
[1 mark]

Question 8 continues on the next page

Figure 9 shows a family tree for the inheritance of cystic fibrosis.

Figure 9

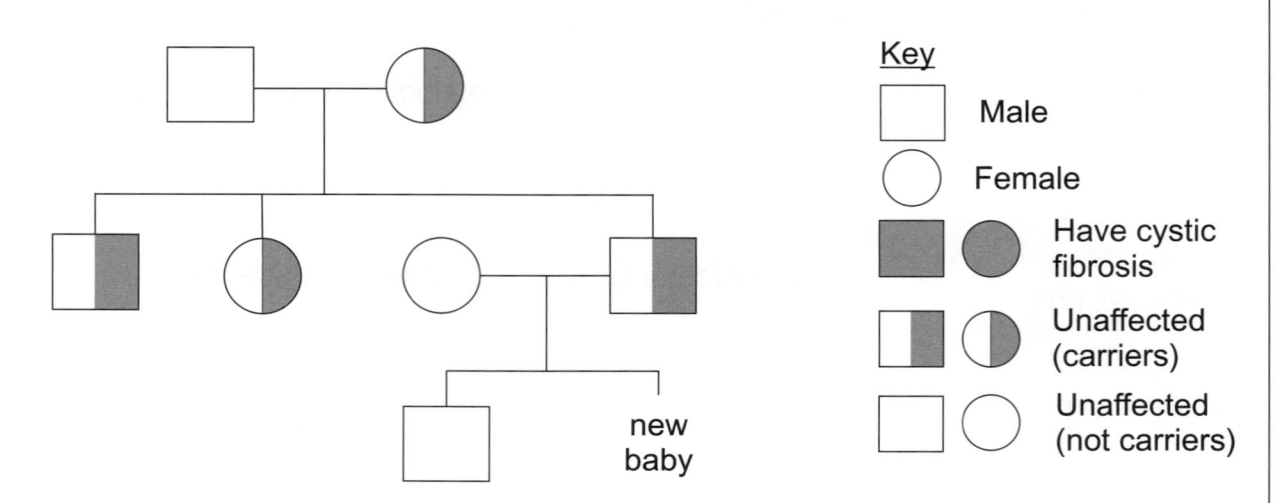

Key
- ☐ Male
- ○ Female
- ■ ● Have cystic fibrosis
- Unaffected (carriers)
- Unaffected (not carriers)

new baby

8.3 Construct a Punnett square to determine the probability of the new baby in **Figure 9** being unaffected and not a carrier of cystic fibrosis.

Use '**F**' to represent a dominant allele and '**f**' to represent a recessive allele.

Probability = ...
[4 marks]

Once the new baby in **Figure 9** is born, the baby's parents decide not to have any more children.

There are many different methods of contraception that they could use to prevent pregnancy. These include the contraceptive implant and the contraceptive injection.

8.4 Compare the contraceptive implant and the contraceptive injection as methods to prevent pregnancy.

....

....

....

....
[2 marks]

8.5 Suggest **two** reasons why a couple may prefer to use methods of contraception such as the contraceptive implant or injection rather than sterilisation.

1. ....

2. ....
[2 marks]

Turn over for the next question

9 Genes are sections of DNA that code for specific proteins.

9.1 Describe how a protein is synthesised in a cell from the code contained in a gene.

....

....

....

....

....

....
[4 marks]

Mutations occur continuously in DNA.

9.2 Explain how a mutation in a gene for an enzyme may influence an organism's phenotype.

....

....

....

....

....

....
[4 marks]

Some sections of DNA are non-coding, which means they don't code for a protein.

9.3 Explain how a mutation in a non-coding section of DNA could affect an organism's phenotype.

....

....

....
[2 marks]

END OF QUESTIONS